THE ETHICS OF TOLERANCE

The Ethics of Tolerance

APPLIED TO RELIGIOUS GROUPS IN AMERICA

By Ira Eisenstein

KING'S CROWN PRESS

MORNINGSIDE HEIGHTS · NEW YORK

1941

TO MY MOTHER AND FATHER

PREFACE

For more than a decade, thoughtful members of the clergy and the laity have been deeply concerned with the problem of improving relations between the various religious groups in the United States. This has been a wholesome development. But the potentialities for good in that development have not been fully realized, partly because the task of creating "good will" has not been approached in the light of a clearly formulated criterion. This criterion I have attempted to present here.

Included in the discussion, among the religious groups, will be found those secular faiths which have sprung up in recent years, and which are still not recognized widely as religions. I believe that their inclusion clarifies many otherwise confused issues.

It is my hope that this essay may advance the cause of religious tolerance—or equity, as I prefer to call it.

Quotations from other works are printed with the kind permission of their respective publishers. I wish to thank the following who have granted this permission:

Harvard University Press, publishers of *Strife of Systems and Productive Duality*, by Wilmon Henry Sheldon; Harcourt, Brace & Co., Inc., publishers of *Reason and Nature*, by Morris Raphael Cohen, and *Freedom: Its Meaning*, edited by Ruth Nansen Anshen; Abingdon-Cokesbury Press, publishers of *The American Canon*, by Daniel L. Marsh; The Macmillan Co., publishers of *The Hope of the Great Community*, by Josiah Royce, and *God in Freedom*, by Luigi Luzzatti; American Council on Public Affairs, publishers of *In Defense of Democracy*, by Frank Murphy; Harper & Bros., publishers of *Catholics, Jews and Protestants*; J. B. Lippincott Company, publishers of *The American Stakes*, by John Chamberlain; The Round Table Press, Inc., publishers of *Intolerance*, by Winfred Ernest Garrison, and *Things That Are Caesar's*, by Paul B. Means; International Missionary Council, publishers of *The Christian Life and Message in Relation to Non-Christian Systems of Thought and Life*; Yale University Press, publishers of *The Nature of the Judicial Process*, by Benjamin N. Cardozo; Charles Scribner's Sons, publishers of *Church and State in Contemporary America*, by Charles Adams Brown, and *The Church and the Political Problem of our Day*, by Karl Barth, and *Moral Man and Immoral Society*, by Reinhold Niebuhr; Little, Brown & Co., publishers of *Of Human Freedom*, by Jacques Barzun; The Vanguard Press, publishers of . . . *Shall Not Perish From the*

Earth, by Ralph Barton Perry; G. P. Putnam's Sons, publishers of *Freedom and Culture,* by John Dewey; Teachers College, Columbia University, publishers of *Theories of Americanization,* by Isaac B. Berkson; The Viking Press, Inc., publishers of *The City of Man: A Declaration on World Democracy;* The John Day Co., Inc., publishers of *All in the Name of God,* by Everett R. Clinchy; and Willett, Clark & Co., publishers of *The American Way,* and *Religious Freedom and Democracy* by Roger W. Straus.

I wish to express my profound thanks to Professor Herbert W. Schneider, of Columbia University, who was of invaluable assistance to me throughout the planning and the writing of this book; to Mordecai M. Kaplan, a true teacher and a constant inspiration; and to Ruth Richards, who prepared the manuscript for publication. None of these should, however, be held responsible for the shortcomings of this work.

August, 1941.   I. E.

CONTENTS

PART ONE

FROM TOLERANCE TO EQUITY

RELIGIOUS TOLERANCE IN AMERICA

The 1920's brought to the United States the first organized efforts to deal with the problem of religious tolerance. The only important effort made before that time to bring together the representatives of various faiths for the purpose of better understanding and the improvement of mutual relations occurred in 1893, when the First Parliament of Religions was held in Chicago, in connection with the Columbia Exposition. According to some, the Parliament served only to set one religion off against another. According to others, it led to increased friendship and understanding among the various religious groups.[1] Whichever estimate of that early convocation is accepted, the fact remains that it was a pioneer effort in the whole field of inter-faith relations. Nothing of consequence developed in that field until the third decade of the twentieth century.

During the first World War, the government had called upon the three major faiths to conduct a joint campaign to raise funds for service to the enlisted men, and coöperation was immediately effected.[2] After the war, however, the Ku Klux Klan and the *Dearborn Independent* (financed by Henry Ford) began to stir up racial and religious hatred. The *American Hebrew*, a Jewish periodical published in New York, countered with articles dealing with better understanding, and combatting religious intolerance. The *Literary Digest* took up the fight; other periodicals joined in.

Organizations were formed to carry on interfaith activities. The World Fellowship of Faiths was established on a permanent basis. The Central Conference of American Rabbis formed a Good Will Committee to coöperate with the similar committee of the Federal Council of Churches of Christ. The Inquiry into the Christian Way of Life was undertaken. Finally, in 1928, the National Conference of Jews and Christians was established, "the only organization of a national character whose sole purpose is the promotion of 'justice, amity, and understanding among Protestants, Catholics and Jews in America.' "[3]

Hopes ran high that religious tolerance was soon to be achieved. There had indeed been "Our Dismal Heritage," as Everett R. Clinchy has referred to it:[4] the long and sorrowful story of religious hatreds reaching back into the beginnings of American history. There had been nativist movements, the Know Nothing movement, the American Protective Association, and the recent revival of the Klan. But faith in America was infinite, and it was hoped that the inevitable progress in material things would be accompanied by parallel progress in spiritual relationships.

Unfortunately, the progress was not as inevitable as Americans had imagined it would be. And in the 1930's a change came over the face of the land. Poverty became a serious issue; intolerance flared up; friction between religious groups developed once again. Perhaps the strongest influence in this change was the violent increase of hatred, bigotry and intolerance in Germany, spreading into the neighboring lands where the Nazis could carry on propaganda and infiltrating into the United States. The rapid increase in religious intolerance came partly through the efforts of paid agitators and partly as a natural reaction to events in Germany.

While the problem became more acute, and people grew more conscious of it than ever before, the weapons for combatting such intolerance multiplied in number and in intensity. The extent of the problem and the extent to which it was being met were, however, extremely difficult to ascertain until 1934, when an admirable study was made by Claris Edwin Silcox and Galen M. Fisher for the Institute of Social and Religious Research. This study was

> undertaken by the Institute of Social and Religious Research at the request of the National Conference of Jews and Christians. This latter organization had been engaged for some time in bringing together representatives of the Protestant, Catholic and Jewish faiths in round-table seminars for mutual discussion and understanding, but had found its educational efforts handicapped by lack of accurate information concerning the actual situations in local communities in contrast with the prevalence of rumor and impression.[5]

The study was as exhaustive as a study of that kind could be, and except for minor changes that have occurred since 1934 the material contained in Silcox and Fisher may be said to describe the situation in the United States today, regarding the relations of Catholics, Protestants and Jews. The areas of conflict are carefully surveyed; they include: Discrimination and Social Distance in Business, Employment and Real Estate, Social Clubs, Political Life and Immigration; Relations in Social Work; Elementary Education, Secondary and Higher Education, and relations to the State; Intermarriage, Conversion and Proselytization. The authors discuss the areas of Coöperation, listing and describing the various organizations and movements devoted to the "growth of tolerance and coöperation."[6]

According to this survey,[7] there were, in 1934, nine organizations carrying on inter-faith work. These fell into two categories: the first included those that

> promote mutual respect among the three faiths and assume their continuing integrity; their motto might be: "coöperation without compromise." They do not ignore differences; indeed, they recognize and almost glory in them. They dwell not on uniformity or combination, but on wealth in variety. . . . In this category belong five agencies: the National Conference of Jews and Christians, the World Fellowship of Faiths, the Religious Education Association, the North American Board for the Study of Religion in Higher Education, and the united religious cabinets of university pastors at Iowa, Cornell, Columbia and the University of California, at Los Angeles. The second category includes those that have a pragmatic object and pay little or no direct attention to creedal matters. In this category belong the occasional coöperation among the social-service organs of the Federal Council, the National Catholic Welfare Conference, and the Central Conference of American Rabbis, . . . the World Alliance for International Friendship through the Churches, the Church Peace Union, the Community Chests, and other intermittent inter-faith activities. . . .[8]

Two types of approach, apparently, have been used. The direct approach involves giving "authentic information" about a group to members of another group in order to correct misapprehensions and false notions. It encourages discussions regarding prejudice, which help to identify prejudice, recognize its falsity, and "replace it by a truer concept." The indirect approach consists of "getting people of different faiths to work together." Through frequent meetings for coöperative effort in behalf of a cause outside themselves, the members of religious groups are to learn gradually

> to adjourn their differences and join hands in worthy enterprises . . . Among the organizations that emphasize this view are the Federal Council of the Churches of Christ, the Religious Education As-

sociation, the Church Peace Union, and the University Religious Conference.[9]

The outstanding organization making use of the indirect approach is the National Conference of Christians and Jews.[10] Its active history is longer than that of any other national body, and the general technique which it fosters is typical of most other organizations, because of its efforts to combine the indirect and the direct approach. To examine its position on the problem of tolerance is therefore of some value.

Its general purpose is to "combat the spirit of intolerance and to take such positive action as . . . [it] could to bring about better understanding amongst the various cultural groups throughout the country."[11] Newton D. Baker defined the purpose of the National Conference of Christians and Jews as follows:

> The N.C.C.J. associates a number of thoughtful and earnest people in an effort to analyze, to moderate, and finally to eliminate a system of prejudices which we have in part inherited and which disfigures and distorts our business, social and political relations.[12]

By means of round-table discussions, good-will tours by priest-minister-rabbi teams, factual studies of the relations of Protestants, Catholics and Jews in American history, the creation of study materials, and other activities, the National Conference of Christians and Jews hopes to further three processes:

> First, the various groups . . . must communicate their aims and ideas to all the members of every other group. Common understanding is necessary for acquaintance and mutual trust. Second, while groups may worship separately, continue their unique traditions, and enjoy their own associations as in a family, all groups must become aware of the fact that all have some aims in common. This is the reason we live together in a community. . . . Third, those mutual aims of American Catholics, Jews and Protestants must be carried into action. In a democratic society all groups must coöperate on common tasks. Illustrations of these tasks are mobilization of religious forces to achieve social and economic justice; to educate for world peace; to deal intelligently with delinquency and crime; to educate for temperance; to cultivate standards of taste in music, architecture, literature, art and the theatre. . . . That, in brief, is the philosophy of the

Round Table of the N.C.C.J. It is not suggesting religious uniformity. The American Way is *E Pluribus Unum*. It is not asking any believer to give up any loyalty, nor to water down any doctrine. It is not comparing one religion with another.[13]

In general, the National Conference may be said to be devoted essentially, (a) to creating, through direct action, a better knowledge and understanding of the various groups by the various groups; (b) through indirect action, to seeking common tasks upon which the various groups can coöperate and "adjourn their differences." This indirect work is based on the assumptions that the friction, hatred, and suspicion that exist between group and group all stem from ignorance and propaganda, and that if the members of the various groups but grew to know one another better they would realize that they all share a belief in "one God who is Creator and Father of all men."[14]

The complete validity of this theory may be seriously challenged. It does not necessarily follow that the better people learn to know one another, the less the friction and hatred between them. Sometimes ignorance breeds tolerance where knowledge would stimulate antagonism.

Nor is it completely true that a common belief in one God is sufficient in itself to create the peace and amity which are desired. The fact is that Americans may share a belief in God, in ethics, even in the Golden Rule, and still differ on those very matters. Roger William Straus, one of the leading figures in the National Conference, quotes Emory S. Bogardus, who enumerates the "factors common to Catholic, Jew, and Protestant." Among these common factors he finds "each group believes in God (definitions may differ). Each believes that ethical elements are essential in religion. Each recognizes the need for religious education. All have social service programs, and emphasize such factors as economic and racial justice, and world peace."[15] Now it may be true that the various religious groups believe in God, but as soon as we add, even in parentheses, that "definitions may differ,"[16] we imply either that the differences of definition are insignificant and not of sufficient importance to quarrel about, or that belief in God itself carries with it no pragmatic implications, for, if it did, one would have the right to assume that the pragmatic implications would vary with the varying definitions.

The same line of reasoning applies to the "ethical elements" in religion. Certainly, religious groups believe that ethical elements are essential in religion; but what does it add to our understanding to mention that fact if the various groups differ in their ethical values? If one group believes that an unhappy marriage should be dissolved, and another believes that divorce is unethical, it means nothing to say that both hold ethical viewpoints.

Similarly, to say that all religious groups recognize the need for religious education does not indicate what kind of education they recognize the need for, nor does it make clear the attitude which we may expect from each group toward, for example, the place of religion in public education, or the responsibility of the public for religious educational institutions. Of a truth, all do have social service programs, and emphasize such factors as economic and racial justice and world peace. But again we have no way of knowing to what extent the common interest in these subjects may make for peace and harmony. The preoccupation with the same vital questions is more likely to create ill will and conflict than the preoccupation with matters that do not touch so immediately upon the security and the well-being of these groups.[17]

In all fairness it must be stated that those who have been participating in the interfaith movement have not been altogether happy about it. They have been conscious of its adequacies. For example, Louis Minsky, writing on "Ten Years of Goodwill",[18] approaches the work of the National Conference with commendable objectivity, pointing out the weaknesses of some of the Conference's early efforts. In the beginning,

the leaders exhibited an excessively sentimental approach. In an effort to atone for past wrongs to Jews and Catholics, Protestants placed too much reliance upon the technique of flattery as a substitute for a scientific approach. The good will movement in its early stages was distinguished largely by its emphasis upon the theme of rabbi loves Christians—minister loves Jews. Sycophantic affirmations of mutual admiration were the order of the day.

Later on, when it became apparent that "in order to eliminate group prejudice, it was necessary to establish the factors which caused it", a new approach was devised, namely, the interfaith seminar. But here too, weaknesses appeared. The leaders confined their efforts to abolishing prejudice based on ignorance. They soon realized, however, that "more constructive results leading to understanding and tolerance come from uniting the three faiths around projects of common interest rather than from unnaturally straining to discuss their religious faiths and practices." Such projects were planned and undertaken. When the totalitarian threat began to occupy their attention more and more, the common task of fighting it constituted a most dramatic common project.

But men like Minsky are quite ready to concede that, despite the excellent work accomplished by the Conference, no clear conception of religious tolerance has yet emerged from the interfaith movement, and that without such a conception, all efforts toward solving this vexing problem to the satisfaction of differing factions are bound at best to result in only momentary palliation.

If organizations like the National Conference of Christians and Jews do not come to grips with the basic issues at stake in inter-faith relations, it is because of the day-to-day functions which they are called upon to perform. When there is a specific job to be done, little time can be taken for a careful and searching scrutiny of the more fundamental problems involved in the issue of religious tolerance. We should, however, expect in the works of those concerned with the question a more thoroughgoing analysis of the entire question of tolerance and intolerance. Yet, in the meager literature that exists on the subject, no success is achieved in setting up a criterion, a norm, by means of which we may judge what shall be tolerated and what shall not. Obviously, tolerance always implies a limit; people will not consent to tolerate the intolerable. What shall be the criterion?

A typical book on the subject is Winfred Ernest Garrison's *Intolerance*.[19] A careful study of the book only leaves the reader with a great number of vague impressions. Intolerance is defined as "the defense that society sets up for the maintenance of its own security against the threatened or supposed dangers from without or within."[20] Again: "The acid test of tolerance in any society is its attitude toward those whose opinions or practices do not conform to the generally accepted standards."[21] When we ask how far society may go in defense of its security, or how far opinions or practices may be tolerated which do not conform to the generally accepted standards, we are told,

> The absolute freedom of individuals is incompatible with the existence of any organized society. Since liberty is always a relative rather than an absolute thing in practice, so also is toleration, but . . . restrictions upon freedom are to go no farther than the exercise of those processes of social control which are essential to the general welfare. . . .[22]

This is obviously argument in a circle. A society is intolerant of anything that threatens its security. Its tolerance is judged by the extent to which it tolerates difference. It cannot be expected, however, to tolerate opinions or practices which are not in accord with the general welfare. The questions still remain: What shall be the fundamental purpose in society? Shall it set up as its objective the secure society, and permit variations of opinion and practice only as concessions by the social group? Shall the state, for example, be the end in itself, and "individual rights" only a privilege? What shall we say to those who contend that we should set up as our objective individual self-expression, and encourage only that type of social organization which is absolutely essential to preserve individuality?

The questions are never answered, and as a result we are left with an appeal to exercise the vague virtues of patience and fair play. The difficulties into which this type of approach leads are apparent as soon as it is applied, as Garrison applies it, to some pressing social problems. For example, in discussing divorce and birth control, it is clear almost immediately that the concept "tolerance" does not contribute to our understanding of the problem.

> Churches which feel that the law . . . has been laid down by revelation can of course do nothing but to maintain an uncompromising position in accordance with what they consider the law of God. . . . For these, intolerance toward divorce and birth control is inevitable, and the term 'intolerance' should be read in this connection with no connotation of reprehensible illiberality. It is a matter of conscience that they should bear their testimony to what they believe to be immutable law of God with reference to human relations. . . .[23]

The problem thus raised is: How can one call upon a person or group to bear with that which is evil? It is difficult to see how one can tolerate that which is intolerable. One is either intolerant of that which is bad or an advocate of that which is good, but tolerance is meaningless. On the other hand, those who are tolerated resent the implication of that term. By virtue of it, they are deemed unworthy and are allowed to continue to function only through the generosity of their tolerators who have the power to put an end to them but who do not exercise that power. Individuals and groups rightly demand justice, not tolerance.

Similarly, with regard to the question of war and peace, Garrison says:

The values involved in this contest of principles are of the utmost importance. They include the greatest human interests, the rights of man, the prosperity and security of the nation, the peace of the world. . . . Tolerance in the sense of pleasant acquiescence on the part of either group toward the other's program is not to be expected. This is not a game, but a struggle. What is proposed by the liberal element amounts to nothing short of revolution . . . and revolutions are neither to be carried through nor put down by a mere smile, or a wave of the hand. That sort of tolerance is out of the question.[24]

What Garrison refers to here is not clear. Certainly, no one defines tolerance as the passive acquiescence in what is considered dangerous. But, on the other hand, he does not help us to understand how far opposition may go before it enters the category of intolerance. When does self-defense cease to be self-defense? How long has one a right to demand that patience shall continue to be a virtue? Unless we are clear in our minds regarding this question, we have no way of distinguishing right from wrong in the category of tolerance.

In an earlier chapter (Chapter II) Garrison attempts to describe what he calls grounds of tolerance. But here too we are left without guidance because he discusses two types of grounds. One type might be called the natural grounds of tolerance, which are merely descriptions of those situations in which we are likely to find the tolerant spirit exercised. Garrison mentions four examples of this type: the case of "good-natured indolence," where "political and social expediency" are involved, where people tend "away from that reliance upon infallible and authoritative absolutes which was characteristic of an earlier age," and where people are indifferent to the issues involved.

With regard to indolence and indifference, which may be coupled, we cannot deny that if a person is too lazy to advocate a point of view, or too indifferent to make an issue of it, no one will raise the issue for him. The tendency away from infallibility also describes a sociological fact, but that ground of tolerance is quite alien to the idea usually associated with the term tolerance. If one is never quite sure of the truth of what one believes, there is no issue of tolerance involved at all. It may be said that to desist from intolerance under such conditions is sheer prudence or expediency. That brings us to the second ground of tolerance listed. While it may be true that under certain circumstances the exercise of tolerance may prove to be expedient, the concept of tolerance generally does not derive from that fact, whatever vague motivation it may have.

The current movements which concern themselves with the program of tolerance do not usually focus upon its practical values. If they did, it would not be necessary to invoke the extraneous qualities of generosity and good will. Unfortunately, however, generosity and good will must be resorted to even where there is the intuition that tolerance is "expedient," because, when the argument of expediency is used, it has no effectiveness unless it is accompanied by precise suggestions. If a program is to depend upon practical effects, it must have some scientific basis.[25] In any event, these are the four examples of that first type of tolerance which Garrison describes. They tell us in a general sort of way the conditions under which we are likely to find what more accurately may be described as the absence of intolerance.

A second type of tolerance which Garrison describes involves values. One example he calls "practical values of diversity. . . . There must be individual variations, or the social group can be neither safe nor prosperous." But he follows this up immediately by asking: "How much variation, and in what respects? That is what we have to find out by experience." Evidently, Garrison is not prepared to formulate any principle. If we have to find the answer to this question by experience, we are likely to stumble along blindly for a long while to come. Unless we are provided with some criterion by which to interpret our experience, or by which to predict consequences, we are likely to suffer much pain and sorrow.

A second example of this second type of tolerance is called "respect for the inalienable rights of man." This principle brings us back to the original difficulty which we have found to be inherent in the usual approach to the problem of tolerance, namely, that the very belief in human rights constitutes one of the sources of resentment against the spirit of tolerance itself. What is a right does not have to depend upon tolerance for existence and recognition. As it is popularly understood, tolerance begins where justice leaves off, and it is that relation of tolerance to human rights which makes it so difficult to define or to conceive clearly the problem of tolerance itself.

A serious attempt to deal with the problem of religious tolerance, and one which commends itself to careful scrutiny, is that of Mordecai M. Kaplan, in his *Judaism In Transition*.[26] The chapter there called "The Meaning of Religious Tolerance" (Chapter IX) approaches the question vigorously. Kaplan quickly arrives at the conclusion that so long as religions depend upon the sanction of revelation, they cannot be tolerant of other religions. Quoting Father Pohle, in the *Catholic Encyclopedia*, to the effect that "the Church of Christ can tolerate no strange churches beside herself, . . . and that outside the Church there is no salvation," Kaplan rightly remarks:

> There is no contesting the logic of the foregoing statement. If we accept the premises, we cannot escape its conclusion. . . . It is therefore necessary for us to go back to the logic of such reasoning to an examination of the premises on which it rests. . . . We must find some other way of establishing the supremacy of the religious ideal with its hope of a humanity united. . . .

He then turns to the theological approach to religion, and finds this equally unsatisfactory because it makes of tolerance just a kind of vague kindliness. "That approach [namely, Philips Brooks's, which Kaplan selects as typical of the theological approach] assumes that all religions seek the truth, but that only our own is a fully satisfying revelation of it. . . . However, we may sympathize with the poor, self-deluded mortals that have not seen the light." Such a conception of tolerance Kaplan finds inadequate because "it denies any validity to those aspects of the other traditions that differ from ours." In other words, the tolerated refuse to be tolerated; they want justice, recognition, acknowledgment of their right to be.

Kaplan then suggests the "psychological approach" which proceeds from the acceptance of the proposition that

> organized religions are integral to particular civilizations and cannot be understood apart from them. . . . What they mean to their own members and what they mean to others can never be the same. . . . Their differences are not merely quantitative variations in the degree of truth that each contains in its tradition, but each is a unique manifestation of the divine, just as each human being is such a unique manifestation. The whole concept of superiority, therefore, falls to the ground.

And with it the whole problem of tolerance, presumably, because intolerance generally depends upon the sense of superiority.

Tracing the origins of religions, and the relation of religions to civilizations, Kaplan elaborates the idea of *sancta*, those "objects, institutions, laws, customs, events and persons that are reverenced by a particular civilization" and that "constitute its religion." Contends Kaplan,

The conception of God which a people or religious fellowship holds, since it is an expression of what that people regards as supremely important, is determined by and expressive of the values that are associated with these sancta or objects of group reverence. This is how different religions are born, and why their true inwardness cannot be communicated. To appreciate the inwardness of a religion fully, one must be conditioned by the totality of the civilization to which the religion belongs. Only then can one realize to what extent a religion is the expression of what the high lights in the life of a people mean to it.

There is the rub: *the conception of God is determined by the values that are associated with the sancta.* As is evident from a study of comparative religions, sancta are sometimes associated with a variety of values, and, conversely, the same values are sometimes associated with the sancta of various religions. When two religious groups, having different sancta, face the same situation, and share the same values, the psychological approach is the perfect approach to a solution of the problem of tolerance. One group can say to the other: "You derive your inspiration for these values from your sancta; I will derive it from mine." But when the values differ as well as the sancta, the element of "superiority" is bound to enter. It cannot be excluded.

Truth, indeed, may be relative, and, as Kaplan says, "what may be true for certain people in certain situations is not necessarily true for others in other situations." But there are times when people of different religions face the same situation at the same time, and they must then insist upon the superiority of their "truth" over the "truth" of their neighbors. Then the differences are really "quantitative variations in the degree of truth. . . ." The proof of this contention is that the problem of tolerance arises practically only when two religious groups, living side by side, face the same situations. When two religious groups in one city of the United States have to face a common problem, such as birth control or divorce, the psychological approach is hardly of help, for as soon as we deal with a conflict of values, we must lapse into the "tolerant" attitude which we find so inadequate. If our values are bound up with what we regard as most sacred to us, we are bound to find opposing values mistaken. We can, of course, grant that those who hold them are sincere and well-meaning, but we must conclude that these people are "poor, self-deluded mortals that have not seen the light." We are, in fact, likely to discover that some of these self-deluded mortals belong to our own religious group, and that they suffer from a false interpretation of the very sancta with which we associate our cherished values.

All in the Name of God[27] is the title of a book by Everett R. Clinchy, a man who has been very active in inter-faith work. In this volume he proposes the solution offered by "cultural pluralism."[28] This phrase connotes "a parity of the different, a democracy of cultures."[29] Clinchy recognizes that

> Catholics will, of course, continue to feel that the Roman Catholic faith is the best, and to them the only true dogma. Protestants will make their affirmations and Jews will make theirs, in accordance with their experience and conviction. There is no reason to expect any lessening of the struggle of ideas and competition of the principles maintained respectively by the three groups. . . . The main change which frank recognition of cultural pluralism in America will bring about is a change in the rules of the game. Good sportsmanship in the combat of cultures is still to be attained. . . . In cultural multiformity, variety, differentiation, lies the secret of the vitality of such unity as the nation or the world may achieve. Cultural growth is best nurtured in the friendly give-and-take, in the normal competition and interplay of citizens by whom cultural pluralism is recognized and accepted. . . . Whether or not a generation can be reared which appreciates that the national life of America as a whole is enriched by the cultural divergences, one group from another, even as the ensemble of a symphony orchestra is more colorful than the single note of a shepherd's flute, remains an open question.[30]

Insofar as Clinchy's proposal touches upon the fundamental problem of homogeneity versus heterogeneity in society, it assumes importance of the first order.[31] Indeed, Silcox and Fisher conclude their extensive survey with the impression that this problem is the most vital one to be faced at the present time.

> The assumption underlying such a [cultural] pluralism is that the true development of man is in the direction not of homogeneity but of heterogeneity, and it is urged in consequence that instead of stressing the melting pot and the obliteration of racial lines, we should encourage the perpetuation of unlikeness and seek a society in which the rights of each cultural variety, however small, to growth and perpetuity, should be frankly recognized. . . . One principle which has

emerged more than once in earlier chapters, as well as in this, is that
the strength and wealth of national life may be enhanced by cherish-
ing within a fundamental unity the cultural richness resulting from
diverse racial and religious heritages. If this principle is sound, it
means not a mere toleration, but positive appreciation of religious
and other cultural variations.[32]

In presenting the concept of cultural pluralism, Clinchy merely
touches upon a momentous question; he does not explore it very far.
Cultural pluralism is spoken of as an opportunity for displaying good
sportsmanship in the combat of cultures. To be sure, good sportsmanship is a fine thing; but when religious groups take their religions seriously, sportsmanship becomes a luxury ill afforded, especially if cherished values are at stake. Furthermore, this "combat of cultures" tends
to defeat the entire purpose of cultural pluralism. The assumption that
cultures may be plural within a society implies the permanence of many
cultures. Combat, since it implies a victory, implies that pluralism is
tentative, to be endured by good sports for the duration of the combat.
"The clash of groups in the United States," says Clinchy, "accounts for
the vitality of the Protestant, Catholic and Jewish movements in this
country."[33] Some Protestants and Jews might question the vitality of
their movements. But, be that as it may, the opponents of cultural pluralism make the point that, of all things, they fear that cultural pluralism will do away with cultural combat. If each group recognizes the
validity of the others, and acknowledges their right to exist and to flour-
ish, nay, realizes the enrichment and the enhancement that derive from
multiple cultures, the likelihood of conflict disappears; even friendly
competition vanishes. Cultural pluralism is based on the assumption
that there cannot be, and that there should be no attempt at, any competition between cultures. Clinchy confuses the issue therefore when he
recommends cultural pluralism because it merely changes the rules,
while retaining the original combat.

On the other hand, to present cultural pluralism merely as enriching
experience is unrealistic. In the first place, there are people who undoubtedly prefer the "single note of a shepherd's flute" to a whole symphony orchestra (or at least to some symphony orchestras). Furthermore,
rich cultural diversity is not always and without exception regarded as
valuable. The question is bound to arise: on what basis is a multiplicity
of cultures to be preferred to a monistic culture? Why, in other words,
choose heterogeneity rather than homogeneity? Certainly, there are

values in homogeneity that cannot be gainsaid. Richness is a desideratum; but shall it be afforded if other values, more important, are sacrificed?

For example, Silcox and Fisher remark that a minority group does

constitute *imperium in imperio;* it must be dealt with often as a separate entity through its leaders; by reason of its cohesion and clannishness and its location at strategic centers, it may exercise a control out of all proportion to its actual numbers, or even its actual contribution to the well-being of society; it does prevent the full and efficient functioning of many social institutions; it raises barriers such as intermarriage to normal social life.[34]

Would Clinchy, if he accepted the description by Silcox and Fisher of the situation that would arise with the existence of ethnic minorities in the United States, insist that the value of "richness" would overbalance all these difficulties?

The editors of the *Christian Century* are certainly not prepared to accept without serious misgivings the values of cultural pluralism. During the months of June and July, 1937, a controversy raged in the columns of that distinguished weekly. The keynote of the controversy was struck clearly in an editorial entitled "Why Is Anti-Semitism?"[35]

The claim of any group to a status as a *permanent* minority is not an obstruction of the democratic process . . ., but something with which Christian feeling cannot help being concerned. This is not alone because Christianity conceives itself as a universal religion and cannot adjust itself to any limitation of its mission short of including all men. It is also due to practical and immediate exigencies. Any group in the cultural life of the community which deliberately insulates itself by nondemocratic [?] barriers against the free movement of the democratic process is inevitably in for bad treatment . . . any group is a social irritant if it insists upon being a *permanent* minority. . . . That doctrine blocks the democratic process. It sanctions cultural separatism. It removes religious values from the free commerce of a dynamic culture. . . . The only religion compatible with democracy is one which conceives itself as universal, and offers itself to all men of all races and cultures. . . . Cultural pluralism is false as a philosophy of the permanent structure of any dynamic society. America's hospitality has already imperiled its democracy. Carried too far, this hospitality results in a society so heterogeneous that it cannot be a community. Too many communities can destroy the community.

Although the editors seem to alternate between a discussion of "religions" and of "cultures," the intent of the editorial, and of those which preceded, and followed it, is clear: heterogeneity is tolerable during the transition to homogeneity.[36] The objective must be homogeneity; the tempo will depend upon the dynamics of American life, upon the willingness of all groups to participate in the interpenetration of faiths and cultures. Whereas Clinchy describes cultural pluralism as "an essential characteristic of genuine democracy at its best,"[37] the *Christian Century* attacks cultural pluralism as a major threat to the democratic process.

How shall we derive guidance and direction, then, from the concept of cultural pluralism as presented? In our search for a criterion of tolerance, we find that tolerance is subordinate to a set of values. When we have clearly fixed the values which we wish to preserve, we know what is tolerable and what is not. Clinchy finds self-realization in the value of diversity, and he pleads with the advocates of homogeneity for "good sportsmanship." The *Christian Century* seems to want an eventual homogeneity; in the meantime, it is willing to tolerate cultural diversity, but how long?

The problem of tolerance today, according to Silcox and Fisher, reduces itself to a very small number of fundamental questions. One of them, homogeneity versus heterogeneity, has been discussed. Another basic issue is authority versus freedom.

The Catholics take their beliefs table d'hote and the Protestants theirs a la carte. . . . The liberal Protestant insists on freedom and rejects authority, and tends to believe that the authority assumed by the church and grounded on alleged facts of doubtful historicity springs less from divine truth than from the skill of political manipulators anxious to enlarge the sphere of their power and authority. To such Protestants, the Catholic doctrine of authority is simply the Nietzschean will to power parading behind a crucifix. . . . The (Protestant) majority (will) ask. . . . "Are we justified in extending the full measure of religious liberty to the Catholic group in the 'name of Protestant principles' when we are far from sure that the Catholic group, were the numerical conditions reversed, would extend the same liberty to Protestants in the 'name of Catholic principles?' Can democracy really endure if one group is educating its children for freedom, while an influential minority in its midst continues to educate its children for authority?"[38]

An unhealthy atmosphere has been created, according to Silcox and Fisher, by the clash of these two principles, authority and freedom; and if "we live together in peace and harmony, it is not because of our respective principles but in spite of them."[39] What has the good-will movement done to reckon with this problem? To what extent have writers on the question taken it into account? Obviously, this problem is not one confined to the Catholic and Protestant religions. It involves the much larger issue which has been agitating people in the democratic countries; (in the nondemocratic countries it is too late for people to be so agitated). The fact that democracy has given way, in one place after another, to the forces of totalitarianism and dictatorship, and the fact that tolerance of antidemocratic ways of thinking and speaking have led to destructive antidemocratic action, have made many otherwise "tolerant" people intolerant altogether of those who advocate, in their way of life, the authoritarian, as opposed to the free, approach. If, then, Protestants suspect Catholics, and the influence that they may wield, they are reflecting in their relation to the Catholics the broader problem of authority versus freedom.

Thomas Mann, writing in the *American Hebrew*,[40] says:

> Democracy's concept of freedom must never include the freedom to destroy democracy; never must it give its deadly enemies that much freedom. If I say this, you will reply: that is the end of freedom. No, I reply, that is its self-preservation. But the very fact that there can be a difference of opinion on this question is proof that freedom is debatable, that it has become a problem.

Thomas Mann is right: freedom has become a problem; in fact, it always has been a problem. And the essence of that problem is the establishment of a criterion of tolerance. People love not only their freedom, though they love that in a special kind of way since it assures them other values which they cherish. But they do cherish other values, and the problem always arises: To what extent shall they resist authority for the sake of freedom; to what extent shall they resist freedom —or exercise authority—for the sake of freedom?

When Protestants, therefore, raise the question concerning Catholics, namely, shall the Catholics be permitted to educate their children for authority, they are raising a question which is equally applicable to communists, Nazis, or any other groups who follow the principle of authority, or the deductive method. How vain it is for the proponents of good will and mutual understanding to whitewash the area of conflict between religious groups, such as the Protestants and the Catholics, by blandly stating that we must bring together "all believers in God, regardless of creed, in a common front against the proponents of intolerance," that basically we all share the same faith! How vain it is, on the other hand, to pretend that true mutual understanding can lead to peace, unless a clearly formulated principle of tolerance is evolved.

We are thus faced with a choice: either the religious groups have basic differences which we must try to ignore, and thus "tolerate", or there are no basic differences, and toleration is not needed. Both of these are unsatisfactory "dead ends." To shut our eyes to realities is to engage in self-deception; sooner or later we shall have to face the realities. On the other hand, to deny the existence of legitimate differences is to fly in the face of facts. We have tried to point out that intolerance does in fact agitate the country at the present time, and that some positive and common basis for inter-faith relations must be found as a practical necessity.

If "religious tolerance" is to mean something concrete which can help to guide the relations between various religious groups, two things are required: first, a better understanding of the theory of toleration in terms of moral principles; and, second, a clearer understanding of the relations between religious societies and of inter-faith issues. The next two sections will deal with these questions respectively.

THE PRINCIPLE OF EQUITY

In this chapter, the thesis is proposed that the principle of equity constitutes the basis for a clear and acceptable criterion by which to measure both the limits of tolerance and the values inherent in it. This principle, applied to our problem, constitutes a fruitful norm for interpreting practical issues in terms of ethical relations already recognized in secular society but peculiarly complicated in matters of religious faith.

While Morris Raphael Cohen is undoubtedly right in saying that the idea of polarity is "as old as philosophy,"[1] the fact remains that social tensions are still represented as logical contradictions and that dialectical method is represented as the only way of dealing with social problems. Josiah Royce made a heroic effort to escape Hegelian dialectic by proving that the three poles in a triadic process of "interpretation" do not necessarily imply antitheses. The relation of polarity is not *ipso facto* a relation of conflict.

> Ethical individualism, [he wrote] has been, in the past, one great foe of the Great Community. Ethical individualism, whether it takes the form of democracy or of the irresponsible search on the part of individuals for private happiness or for any other merely individual good, will never save mankind. Equally useless, however, for the attainment of humanity's great end would be any form of mere ethical collectivism. . . .[2]

A more explicit formulation of the idea of polarity related to the present problem is that of Wilmon Henry Sheldon.[3]

> Every practical problem, [he wrote], should in our belief be met thus: of the two positions in conflict, ascertain by empirical analysis which one represents the principle of externality, and which that of internality; seek a solution which will identify the interest of each factor, yet so as to leave room for the pursuit, on occasion, of each one by itself.[4]

Sheldon explains, earlier in his work, that "internality" refers to an entity in relation to other entities; "externality" in relation to its own structure and function. Thus, for example, when a problem arises which involves reason versus authority, or individualism versus "socialism," the polar quality of the situation must be thoroughly appreciated. The "ideal rule" to follow is that which effects "the organic fusion of the two counter-motives which make up human society."[5] Sheldon believes that "productive duality," as he calls it, should constitute the foundation of ethics: "a sound ethics must be based upon metaphysics; for we shall never know how to adjust ourselves to our great environment until we know the nature of that environment"; and he devotes several hundred pages to demonstrating that the true description of reality is that which recognizes the polarity inherent in all relations.

In a particularly prophetic passage, he foresees, for example, the dangers of leaning too far to the side of "socialism," or the neglect of individualism.

To every age its own premises seem final; and in this age, even to the most intellectual men of it, the democratic principle, with exclusive emphasis upon the social relations, and the principle of internality, seems the goal of all human effort and the absolute truth of life. Yet it is not becoming to the thinker to be carried off his feet by a partisan view. He should learn the lesson of history, that the pendulum is bound to swing from one side to the other, that a one-sided type must sooner or later be corrected by its counter-type. It is not possible that the internal principle will finally shut out the external [in other words, that coöperation, totalitarianism, will finally shut out individualism]. In the latter, the former meets its crucial point: which is to say that certain natural instincts of man can never be erased nor quenched by the doctrine that man is only a member of society. Man is more than a network of relations. Members differ, each is bound to retain a measure of independence. He must be allowed, if he can, to see further than the public conscience of his time, see, to develop perhaps, in some isolation the fruits of his own personality, whether in the way of artistic production or scientific discovery or religious insight. . . . Much trouble may be saved if we reflect that individualism cannot be extirpated from our nature. Any student of philosophical systems who has seen human thought try one reform after another should know that this oscillation between extremes only perpetuates the battle. The bitter conflict persists, and always will persist, until some harmonizing principle is brought to bear.[6]

The recent attempts of Royce, Cohen, and Sheldon are cited to revive the concept of polarity in social analysis because a clear understanding of polar tension is basic to an understanding of equity as a social norm. Both the idealistic and the materialistic versions of collectivism have adopted a dialectical methodology, and dialectic is based on the idea of struggle, incompatibilities, contradictions. Where struggle is basic, the outcome is victory, defeat, or compromise—not conciliation. A theory of conciliation demands different categories. The philosophies of individualism, on the other hand, have also relied on the concepts of competition, independence, "like liberties," and similar atomistic notions to define social relations. On such bases, tolerance can be conceived of only as compromise, or as the *Catholic Encyclopedia* puts it, "patience with evil." The doctrine of equity or justice has fared badly. "Fair competition," for example, is difficult to define, theoretically as well as practically; if it is fair, it is not competition, and if it is competition, it is not fair. On such bases a "mean state", or state of equilibrium, is not easily represented as a virtuous state.

The relation of polarity, and the corollary state of equilibrium, form the basis for a theory of tolerance as a virtue. In these terms, tolerance or equilibrium can be defined as that state in the relations between a social group and any part within it, or between groups, which is achieved when two or more separate forces or poles continue to move ahead, being productive rather than disturbing factors for each other, without forming an organic unity. Social equilibrium, in other words, implies two functions, one centrifugal and one centripetal, which are mutually sustaining rather than conflicting. For purposes of social analysis, let us call these functions individuality and coöperation. "Individuality" may be expressed by any living unit in a community, whether consisting of one person, institution, organization, or movement, or of a number of such units. "Coöperation" refers to the "division of labor" or other forms of reciprocity in a community. Like individuality, it too may consist of a small group, like the family, or of as large a group as mankind. The same group can represent "individuality" or "coöperation," depending upon its functioning. Thus a family represents coöperation in relation to one child in it; on the other hand, it represents individuality in relation to the community. An individual or group is said to be equitable or in equilibrium with another when both these functions are being promoted. Individuality and coöperation are obviously not necessarily antithetical or conflicting; they may or may not be compatible.

The aim of equity is to define the conditions under which they are compatible.

The conception of polarity upon which the principle of equity is built has little in common with the idealistic notions about the dialectics of history. The poles of individuality and coöperation are not to be confused with the "thesis" or the "synthesis" of Hegel. Nor is the relation between part and whole to be interpreted as that which obtains between thesis and antithesis; for example, there is no necessary progression to synthesis, and when the interaction of part and whole takes place, we are not left merely with synthesis. Both poles remain to function. The dynamics of this polarity are therefore, in a sense, static. As a matter of fact, to absorb the poles into one another in order to achieve a synthesis would be to do violence to the very ethical ideal which has been set up. Nor is any attempt made here to suggest that the whole is more "real" than the part, or vice versa. The idealistic teaching that the totality enjoys greater *reality* than any part thereof plays no role in this discussion.

The problem of tolerance arises when the interests of individuality and those of coöperation are both taken into consideration, and need to be reconciled. When either one or the other of these functions suffers neglect, the equilibrium is upset, and intolerance may be said to constitute the result. One kind of intolerance, for example, is "self-defense" or "self-preservation." This is bound to ensue when one or the other unit cannot "tolerate" the situation any longer, because it must either fuse with another or injure another. A disturbance of equilibrium in the interests of self-preservation must, however, be carefully distinguished from a similar disturbance motivated differently: by a unit that masquerades as the guardian of others, or that falsely represents its activities as self-defense. This type will be referred to later.

When the safety or the integrity of others is challenged by any unit, or, in other words, when the increase of individuality threatens to affect the functioning of coöperation, the natural reaction on the part of the others is to limit the scope of individuality in order to restore the balance. Thus, a government may equitably curtail the rights of citizens when a condition of emergency arises which involves a threat to the individuality and integrity of each. If, on the other hand, the government encroaches by its activities upon the functions actually being performed in the direction of individuality a reaction intended to curtail that tendency will sooner or later take place.

Tolerance[7] is the term that we should apply to that condition of equilibrium which exists when one and all are "tolerably" satisfied with their reciprocal effects on each other. This does not mean that they have no conflicting interests. It does mean, however, that the interests are able to continue in conflict without destroying each other, for example, "sporting" competition. This type of tolerance should be called natural tolerance. Natural tolerance can be of two kinds: in one kind the relation of individuality and coöperation is static, each pole functioning without any particular reference to the opposite pole, passively accepting it and finding no cause for upsetting the equilibrium. It presupposes approximate equality. This is the type of equilibrium, or state of tension, which a writer like Chamberlain[8] suggests for the proper functioning of a democracy. For him, democracy consists essentially in the maintenance of equilibrium between the various parts of a whole, in such a way that no part attempts to become the whole.

> Democracy, [he writes] is only possible in a society of various groups and classes, a society of many available alternatives. . . . If their power is evenly spread, if there are economic checks and balances to parallel the political checks and balances, then society will be democratic. For democracy is what results when you have a state of tension in society that permits no one group to dare bid for the total power. . . .[9] I want to hymn the virtue of a mixed economy, an eternally pluralistic economy, not in terms of presenting an argument for chaos, or the status quo, but in terms indicating the proper components of a permanently workable, dynamic balance.[10]

From Chamberlain's discussion, it is not clear whether he refuses to reckon with the *whole* as a pole in the tension, and reckons only with a series of parts, or whether he assumes that each part is in tension with all the rest that constitute the whole. It is also not clear in what sense he uses the term "dynamic" as applied to "balance."

Barzun, also, speaks of democracy in terms of equilibrium.[11]

> Freedom, or Free Democracy, is something very different and much more difficult to achieve. It is a balance between the popular will and individual rights. It is a civilized society that tries to establish diversity in unity through the guarantee of civil liberties. It wants stability and peace, but recognizing the dynamic character of society it finds it must safeguard criticism as sacred and insure the free expression of thought as an Intellectual Privilege granted equally to all.[12]

Here, too, it is not quite clear in what sense the word "dynamic" is used. If Barzun means constantly changing and growing, he uses it in a sense somewhat different from what I have in mind. In this section, I retain the term "static" equilibrum to describe the kind of equilibrium maintained in a condition of tolerance when the polar entities have not necessarily a creative or dynamic relation between them, although the society in which that equilibrium occurs is dynamic.

The second type of natural tolerance may be called dynamic in the sense that the units enjoy more than the mere freedom from outward compulsion and that their coöperation enjoys more than the absence of need to exercise outward compulsion. From the point of view of dynamic natural tolerance, there is a state of equilibrium when each of the poles creates those conditions which make for the realization of the potentialities of the opposite pole. As Sheldon puts it:

> The free union of two produces a third . . . the ideal of the state is the union of individualist and social motives in which each, so to speak, fertilizes the other; the good citizen's individuality being developed by his citizenship, and conversely.[13]

Thus mutual fructification and reciprocal enrichment result from the interaction of the poles, and from the consequent realization in each of its respective highest potentialities.[14] We might call this type of natural tolerance *creative* tolerance, by virtue of the effect that it has upon each of the poles.

An interesting application of the theory of reciprocal relations between individuality and coöperation appears in several statements in *The City of Man,* a recent declaration by a group of scholars, writers, and teachers.

> It is true that the value of the individual person is ultimate and that the democratic community, unlike the all-devouring totalitarian state, must be ordained to promote the welfare and fulfillment of each person. But it is equally true that no individual good life can be lived outside a good society, and that the single citizen must strive toward a common good which is beyond him as it is beyond any single community and any passing generation. Here . . . the centralizing and the peripheral drives are indispensable to each other.[15]

There is, however, an altogether different type of approach to tolerance which yields ethical tolerance or equity. Natural tolerance can be observed objectively as can any physical equilibrium. Ethical tolerance, on the other hand, implies the attempt to create equilibrium consciously by using norms of conduct in social relations. Ethical tolerance is dynamic equilibrium achieved deliberately. It implies the acceptance of the ideal of equity and the belief that the moral good consists in social institutions and habits which make individuality and coöperation not only compatible but reciprocally stimulating.

The ethical norm may be stated as follows: That is equitable which makes the poles of coöperation and individuality fruitful for each other. Thus ethical tolerance may be identified as the conscious fostering of creative or dynamic polarity. Ethical tolerance does not create resentment in the tolerated because the tolerated is, in this relation, not regarded by the tolerator as a necessary evil. Secondly, in ethical tolerance the relationship is reciprocal, and each tolerates the other insofar as each has nothing to fear from the other. But even more, there is in ethical tolerance the incentive to cultivate individuality for the sake of the whole, and coöperation for the sake of the part, by reason of the enrichment which each provides the other. When a kind of enlightened self-interest dictates ethical tolerance, a sound foundation has been laid. Enlightened self-interest is not to be confused with ordinary expediency. Expediency implies that a certain procedure is to be preferred at a particular time, under particular circumstances, which under normal conditions would be regarded as wrong. Ethical tolerance implies that the procedure it represents is both fitting and good. It is virtuous, not in the sense that it runs counter to some natural tendency to which human beings wish to regard themselves as superior, or which in their desire to be truly human they attempt to transcend. Ethical tolerance is expedient, not under special circumstances but under most circumstances.

What are the prerequisite conditions for such tolerance? How long has one a right to demand equity? The answer is: One has a right to demand equity so long as there is no imminent danger that either pole tends to destroy the other. The purpose of tolerance is clear. We now know when tolerance is useful and when it is harmful, and we have a criterion for judging what should be tolerated and what should not.

This principle of ethical tolerance may be compared with a similar one recently set forth by Ralph Barton Perry, who, in his little volume entitled . . . *Shall Not Perish From the Earth*,[16] enunciates the principle of "libertarianism as an end" as opposed to "libertarianism as a scruple." The advocate of tolerance, says Perry, faces a dilemma.

Either he must deny liberty for the sake of preserving it, or he must tolerate liberty with a full knowledge that in effect he will have denied it. This apparent dilemma rests, however, upon a confusion between two kinds of libertarianism. There is a libertarianism of scruple, and a libertarianism of end; and the dilemma is escaped by the explicit and steadfast adoption of the one or the other.

The libertarianism of scruple is "acceptance of tolerance as an absolute and inviolable maxim." Libertarianism as an end, however, "is concerned with creating a set of social institutions in which liberty is realized," and resorts, if necessary, even to "the momentary or partial suppression of liberty."

Perry offers two possibilities, neither of which is philosophically satisfying. The libertarianism of scruple is, of course, unacceptable, for the obvious reasons which he presents. It leads to sheer anarchy. The alternative, however, is equally unsatisfying because, although Perry tries to make a principle out of it, it is essentially a recourse to compromise. The curtailment of liberty is presented as an evil necessary for the salvaging of some liberty from the wreckage of cataclysmic events. The opposite pole of liberty is, in other words, purely negative. Perry constantly refers to individualism as the sole value. Whatever curtailment of individualism he advocates he conceives as a concession, a reduction of a good. Restraint, according to him, is always bad but must be suffered sometimes in the interests of the ultimate good, of individualism. Thus Perry underestimates the positive values of coöperation in his discussion of tolerance. "Public order" seems to be the only positive good that the whole can provide.

The principle here submitted conceives of vast possibilities for good in coöperation, values which are not only not inconsistent with individuality but which render individuality itself more secure and enriched. Thus ethical tolerance resolves the dilemma of scruple versus end by making them coincident. The tolerance of a scruple is that which sets up equity as its ethical objective.

The question is, in view of the important difference between the connotation of "tolerance" as it is popularly used and the connotation here submitted, whether it is fitting that the same word should be retained for the new connotation. Should we not replace it with one that is better suited to our needs? This problem arises every time an important transition occurs in social processes. Inherited terminologies which include such as "God," "religion," "church," "family," "home,"—so-called halo words, have become so grooved in people's consciousness that they continue to be used even after the values with which they were originally identified are forsaken. The tendency generally is to reinterpret old words in terms of new values. There is much to be said for this procedure. It helps to maintain the cultural continuity of the group and satisfies the need for investing with prestige ideas which otherwise might sound revolutionary. On the other hand, there is always the danger that the continued use of the same terms may obscure the more precise meanings which they have begun to assume. Further, it is a very long and difficult process to dissociate new meanings of words from their original connotations in the minds of the masses of people.

The analysis of "tolerance" and the inquiry into the natural basis for a clearly formulated concept, one that would be both creative and directive, raise the question of the advisability of retaining that term, which is so closely wed to its old sentimental and ambiguous connotation. If the term "tolerance" had ever been a satisfactory term, and if it had pleasant and wholesome associations there would be some value in retaining the term. But it differs from the halo words in that it has never satisfied the parties who stood in the relation of tolerance.

Because, on the one hand, it is unrealistic to assume that one can arbitrarily exile a word from the realm of common usage, and because, on the other hand, the term is so unsuited to the clarified meaning here outlined, the term tolerance should, therefore, be retained only to describe the *natural phenomenon of social polarity.* "Tolerance" should be used to describe that condition of social equilibrium which exists when there is no conscious striving for equilibrium. *When, however, there is an awareness of the relations, and attempts are made to ascertain how those relations should be altered, or when the question of deliberate action is involved, we should speak of "equity" and not of "tolerance."*

"Equity" has several advantages. First, it establishes the relation between the parties involved as coördinate rather than as the relation of a greater to a lesser or a stronger to a weaker. The term "tolerance," even when the word "ethical" is attached to it, still gives the impression that the tolerated stands on a lower level than the tolerator. A corollary follows from this first advantage, namely, that because there is coördinate relation there is possibly a reciprocal relation. In "equity" one can discern the possibilities of dynamic equilibrium consciously pursued; in the concept "tolerance" one looks for this in vain. "Equity" has noble associations in the field of law. Equity in law always seeks to maintain the equilibrium between individuality and coöperation, the part and the whole, or one part and another part of society, on the basis not of the literal adherence to a code but of a flexible interpretation of the relative moment of conflicting claims.[17]

This discussion of the polar relations between the one and the many, the part and the whole, individuality and coöperation, might be misleading if certain important considerations were not clarified. For example, Chamberlain, in the book cited above, referred to a "pluralistic" economy, implying that the equilibrium that constitutes the essence of democracy is an equilibrium not between any two poles but among a variety of poles, so to speak, in a pluralistic and variegated group containing many parts, each with its own interests and aspirations. Here confusion is likely to occur. The "pluralism" of which pluralists speak does not exclude the polarity of which I speak. Certainly, every group, no matter how small, represents a plurality of individualities within it, but together, and insofar as they constitute a group or are regarded and are prepared to regard themselves as a group, there is a community in which all the individualities participate in common. The relation between this community and any individuality within it constitutes a polarity.

Further, we must make clear that the problem of equity arises just as frequently between one part and another part as it does between the part and the whole; notwithstanding this, the principle of equity operates, because even when there is a tension between part and part, in reality there is also tension between these parts and the community which includes them.

For example, in the social unit A there are among others two parts, X and Y. The relations of X and Y are determined, speaking from the point of view of natural tolerance, by the fact of polarity. When the equilibrium between them is maintained, it indicates that the two parts stand in a relation to one another equivalent to the relation that exists between the part and the whole in a condition of natural tolerance. But if conflicting interests should happen to develop to the point where the equilibrium might be upset, part X finds it necessary to identify its interests with the interests of A.

In the course of most social processes, no part attempts to oppose another part with the avowed purpose of advancing its own cause. If a part actually believes that its interests are identical with the interests of the whole, it presents its cause as the cause of the whole. As soon, then, as part X in its opposition to part Y identifies itself with A we find ourselves dealing again with the relation of the whole to the part. The success or failure of X depends upon X's ability to prove to A that the actions of Y are dangerous not only to the integrity of X, but also to that of A. If X fails to persuade A by legitimate means that the actions of Y are dangerous, X will get no support from A and will have either to content itself with the measure of individuality that it already enjoys or to resort to some illegitimate means of convincing A that it is in peril from Y.[18]

The second alternative creates what might be called artificial intolerance. The part X does not merely fail to realize the existent possibilities for reciprocal enrichment; what is worse, it attempts to upset the equilibrium by raising false issues and arousing unwarranted fear. In most instances, artificial intolerance is induced by exaggerating the extent to which individuality may be said to encroach upon coöperation, or, conversely, the extent to which coöperation may be said to encroach upon individuality. In a larger sense, this artificial or unwarranted intolerance constitutes one of the major problems of society. As we have seen, in the natural course of events equilibrium is often upset because individuality or coöperation is jeopardized, and the reaction that ensues is merely a form of self-defense or self-preservation. But when the upset of equilibrium is not related to self-defense, we are faced with a force that is defeating the ends of "equity."

The generation of unwarranted fear is due, usually, to either of two causes: one of these is ignorance. The other is malice. Ignorance may result from the absence of facts or the possession of the facts in distortion. Ignorance may instil in a part a fear of the whole, which will precipitate actions in self-defense when the danger is remote or even nonexistent. The action intended as defense then becomes interpreted as offense and sets into operation defense activities by the opposite pole, thus upsetting the equilibrium. We must not, however, fall into the fallacy of imagining that equilibrium can always be achieved through mutual understanding and through the increase of knowledge. Though ignorance is frequently the cause of unwarranted intolerance, it may very often happen that the lack of fear by the whole of any part in it may be due to the very ignorance by the whole of the true character and intentions of the part. It may very well be that in some instances the whole would react violently to the part, and the coöperation would seek to curtail the individuality, if the whole were fully aware or had a thorough knowledge of the facts relating to the part. There are times, in other words, when ignorance helps to retain the blissful equilibrium.

The fact remains, however, that whereas knowledge may sometimes upset the equilibrium, ignorance is the more prevalent cause. This ignorance may again be due to different causes. It may be due to original negligence, or to criminal methods—deliberate and studied. When knowledge is lacking or denied, social evils may result; that is criminal negligence. But when lies are maliciously spread and false propaganda disseminated, we have criminal deliberation, artificially cultivated ignorance, which in turn generates fear for the unity and integrity of either the part or the whole, resulting in the inequitable upset of equilibrium, or artificial intolerance.

The second cause of artificial intolerance is malice and is to be distinguished from that caused by ignorance by the fact that malice refers to those who deliberately falsify the facts so that others shall be ignorant of their true character. The first refers to those who are themselves ignorant. Our faith in equity rests upon the belief that malice once exposed will tend to destroy itself. Without that assumption, we face a chaotic world in which no moral objective can possibly be achieved. This basic faith in human beings is indispensable for our purpose. Yet so long as malice and ignorance continue to function, and while efforts are made to counteract them, social units and parts thereof, for the sake of their own integrity, must realize that it is to their best interests to effect such techniques as are best calculated to defer, for the longest possible time consistent with safety, the operation of fear which is responsible for acts of intolerance.

There are many advantages in postponing for the longest possible time the disturbance of the equilibrium in self-defense. If exaggerated fear or panic can be avoided, time is gained. While there is time there is opportunity to avoid the cumulative evils of internecine strife. It has already been indicated how a step in self-defense interpreted as an offensive may lead to social cataclysm. Time has a strange way of resolving conflicts. Sometimes they solve themselves; sometimes they fade into insignificance in the face of larger problems. Time provides opportunity for negotiation. Negotiation can uncover the causes of conflict and ascertain whether there is malice involved or whether ignorance is at the root of the matter. Negotiation leads to a better understanding of the true character of the tension, and establishes the needs of both parties for their self-realization. An awareness of the principle of equity, based upon polarity, will therefore constitute a major incentive to negotiation. But even more: because negotiation is one of the most creative instruments for effecting equity, we may infer that just as equity, from this analysis, becomes the criterion of conduct and the norm of judgment, so the willingness to enter into negotiation is a criterion of adherence to this norm. Negotiation is the inevitable corollary of the acceptance of equity. By that token, the refusal to negotiate may be identified as the sign of artificial intolerance (as distinct from "natural" intolerance). It is reprehensible because the individual or group, in refusing to negotiate, assumes by implication that its individuality is incompatible with coöperation. That this assumption is implied is clear from the fact that negotiation, as the instrument of equity, proceeds from *its* assumption that individuality is to be preserved—and, in fact, fostered. The refusal to negotiate cannot therefore be based upon the claim of "self-defense" unless we infer that, according to this individual or group, its "self-preservation" is endangered by any and all forms of coöperation. Thus, the intolerance which results is reprehensible because it denies dynamic equilibrium and thwarts the purposes of equity.

It is necessary to point out that situations may arise in which two parts of the same whole may temporarily be unmindful of mutual conflicts and unite against the whole in order that each may strengthen its claim to individuality by alliance with the other.[19] For example, part X and part Y, fearing the encroachment upon their individuality by the whole A, might stress coöperation between themselves for the sake of the individuality which each desired. This stress upon coöperation might momentarily upset the equilibrium so that the individuality of each might actually be submerged in their local coöperation. This, however, might be necessary at the time to establish the larger equilibrium. Thus we have the paradox of parts X and Y forgetting their individuality, emphasizing their coöperation in the interests of their common opposition to A, which represents absolute coöperation, in order that they may ultimately achieve their respective individuality in relation to A.

What is the bearing of all this on the vital problem which we have posed: homogeneity versus heterogeneity? The answer should be clear: *The choice is a fallacious and misleading one. From the principle of equity we should derive an understanding of the absolute necessity of both heterogeneity and homogeneity.* We need homogeneity for coöperation and heterogeneity for individuality. Cultural pluralism as described by Silcox and Fisher, in terms of a predominance of heterogeneity, certainly deserves the censure they give it. As a matter of fact, they present cultural pluralism in a bad light giving it the European form. This form of cultural pluralism not only failed in Europe but was criticized a long time ago by Berkson in his *Theories of Ameri-canization*.[20]

> The simplest and therefore most telling objection to this type of governmental organization for the United States is the recognition that it is a notion imported from foreign conditions without realizing that the very considerations which make it valid there are totally different in this country.[21]

Berkson would agree completely with Silcox and Fisher that the kind of cultural pluralism which makes an *imperium in imperio* out of each individuality is objectionable. That is not what Clinchy has in mind at all. His theory is more closely related to that which Berkson offers as the alternative to Kallen's Federation of Nationalities program, namely, the Community Theory.

According to this theory, foreign ethnic groups would be perpetuated in the United States. It is not based

> upon any demonstration of the value of the cultural contribution that any such group might make [here Berkson goes beyond Clinchy] but upon the right to life, and expression of personality inherent in the nature of the individual. . . . In a democracy, no demonstration of value is needed precedent to permitting either an individual or a group to live . . . Life justifies itself. It is the suppression of life that needs justification. Indeed, if it is clearly shown that the presence or activities of any particular group cannot be continued except at the expense of other groups, or of the total group, then its activities must be restrained within just bounds, or altogether eliminated when there is no other way out. However, when no impartial demonstration of the evil effects of the presence of any ground is possible, then "tolerance" must be Democracy's rule. . . .[22]

Berkson bases his theory upon the "inherent" right to life which an individual or group has by virtue of its very being. He thus came close to establishing an ethical criterion or norm without actually articulating it. His reference to "inherent" rights exposes his argument to all the contradictions involved in the theory of natural rights. The critique of natural rights by those who see in society the struggle for power immediately confuses and involves the issue. If Berkson, instead of regarding the whole or the "total group" as an entity in static relation to diverse parts, had reckoned with the dynamic and creative polarity between part and whole, he would have been able to express his case for the Community Theory (which is merely another name for cultural pluralism) in terms of an ethical norm based upon a natural or sociological phenomenon.[23]

In the same way that Berkson deals with the Federation of Nationalities theory, he deals with the "Americanization" theory, which is what the *Christian Century*, in substance, presents. Here we have the reverse side of the medal. Americanization means homogeneity; homogeneity *alone* violates the principle of equity. In fact, if the principle of homogeneity were to be applied to its logical conclusion, it would mean the end of democracy altogether. *Totalitarianism is the reductio ad nauseum of homogeneity.*

The claim that cultural pluralism, applied to universal creeds, would involve the surrender of universalism in those creeds is equally untenable.[24] In every event a polarity is observable. In every culture there is the duality of particularism and universality. The universality of a religion inheres in the truths it teaches which are universally applicable. The particularism inheres in the form in which those universal truths are couched.[25] Every cultural phenomenon of high quality evolved out of the particular experience of a particular segment of the human race. In no case has universalism of appeal been affected by particularism of language, tradition, form of expression.

When cultural pluralism, therefore, is spoken of as incompatible with universalism, a serious mistake is made. In a culturally pluralistic whole, each part would seek to be universal in ethical values and particular in form, just as the various nationalities in the Soviet Union are supposed to be "socialist" in content and "national" in form. In a culturally pluralistic society each group would seek to influence, and to fructify and enrich the other by the dissemination of those ethical values which it would want the rest to adopt, and each in turn would be enriched by its exposure to the totality of the others. In this reciprocal and dynamic relation, polarity would function. Each element, and the whole itself, would be guided by the ethical norm.

Now, the questions arise: What should be done to those who do not accept the principle of equity? What about those who do not want democracy, but who wish to use it for the purpose of abolishing it? What about those who demand the right to individuality only that they may do away with individuality by becoming the whole, and insisting upon conformity from all the parts? What about those who teach

authority and not freedom? Are they not violating equity by starting
from the assumption that nothing can be learned from others, that the
only function the others have is to learn from them?

Here the principle of equity comes to its own rescue. On the one hand,
there are those who maintain that freedom should be granted only to
those who believe in it. On the other hand, there are those who cannot
condone the curtailment of freedom in any area on the ground that
once freedom is denied to some it no longer exists: people should have
unlimited freedom. Both these extremes reckon without the principle
of equity. This criterion, applied to the problem of those who reject it,
will result in the following conclusion: the rejection of the principle
of equity must be regarded as a manifestation of individuality. We must
take cognizance of the fact that there are some who sincerely and con-
scientiously believe that any kind of freedom is an unmitigated evil;
that the individual counts for nothing; that the group is the only value
worth preserving and advancing. It is true that this particular individuality is by nature inconsistent with equity, in the sense that it refuses
to accept the idea of polarity and hence denies the essential prerequisite
for equity. Nevertheless, we must place it in the same category with other
kinds of individuality, for the moment we set up, a priori, the types of
acceptable individuality, and decide in advance which can be rendered
compatible with coöperation and which cannot, we are not only violating ethical tolerance, we are impeding even natural tolerance.

When, therefore, those who do not believe in democracy (in a democratic nation) are not sufficiently dangerous to threaten the integrity of
the whole, they should be tolerated. In fact, they should be encouraged
to articulate their individuality to the greatest possible degree, provided
that this articulation is achieved by means of honest self-expression.
(This question is further explored below.)

Thus shall be done to all those who teach authority and not freedom,
who teach children to believe that they must mold their lives and their
conduct in accordance with a pre-established code enjoying authority,
instead of in accordance with social objectives such as life, liberty, and
the pursuit of happiness. If the prevailing opinion in the group favors
the inductive approach, those who differ should be given full opportunity to exercise their individuality, so long as the equilibrium is not
upset, so long as the integrity of the group is not jeopardized.

The fact is, however, that the problem of authority versus freedom is
not quite so clear-cut as Silcox and Fisher would have us believe. It is true
that among certain groups resort to authority is practiced as the normal

procedure. But as a matter of fact those groups which guide themselves by authority do not practice the deductive method to the extent that they seem to. Insofar as there is development discernible in their history, some amount of trial and error must have seeped in. The process of interpretation satisfies the need for sanction, but in reality interpretation generally takes cognizance of the new conditions that must be met, and freedom is exercised. If it pleases the orthodox to believe that the innovations they are instituting are only the explicit application of what is implicit in the text, nobody need protest.[26]

On the other hand, not everyone who believes in trial and error practices that exclusively either. Respect for tradition, for precedent, for continuity with the past, natural conservatism—all these tend to temper trial and error and make for the setting up of hypotheses and accepted norms which are used as checks against rash innovations. Once again we must revert to our principle of polarity. There is a constant dualism in all social acts: they are decided upon in the light of accepted hypotheses and then constitute inductive evidence as correctives to these hypotheses. In science, this is going on all the time. In law, says Cardozo, "as in every other branch of knowledge, the truths given by induction tend to form the premises for new deductions,"[27] and he quotes Munroe Smith to the effect that the "rules and principles of case law have never been treated as final truths, but as working hypotheses. . . . If the accepted rule which seems applicable yields a result which is felt to be unjust, the rule is reconsidered."[28]

It is therefore somewhat disingenuous for members of one religious group to speak of another religious group as being addicted completely to the deductive or authoritarian method, as contrasted with their own group, which is committed to the inductive or free method. From the point of view of polarity, all groups use both. Some, it is true, lean more toward authority; others more toward freedom. But that is true of all people: some are more conservative and others more progressive. What we frequently forget is that even among those who judge entirely by the standards of life, liberty and the pursuit of happiness, there is enormous difference of opinion.

Now we must proceed to investigate the area in which the norm of equity is to be applied if we are to come to a clear understanding of the problem of religious tolerance. We must, in other words, define the scope of the term "religious", as applied to the American scene with which we are concerned. Which are the religious groups in the United States? How are they to be identified? This problem will occupy us in the chapter that follows.

PART TWO

THE PRINCIPLE OF EQUITY APPLIED

CONTEMPORARY FAITHS

In order to approach the problem of religious tolerance realistically, in terms of contemporary American society, we must examine the various faiths which are represented on the scene. When we have done this, we will have some notion of the scope of the problem and of the precise character of the conflicts which constitute the problem.

Contemporary America is the scene of conflicting and competing systems of salvation. Among these are the so-called nonreligious state, the Catholic Church, or Church-State, the Protestant Christian denominations, the Jewish religion, and the groups espousing secular faiths, such as communism, Nazism, and other minor groups. These are all to be regarded as social groups offering salvation to their adherents. The language used in each case is not the most important consideration determining whether they all belong in the same category or not. The so-called secular faiths are to be treated as religious groups when they achieve a degree of intensity and symbolization which in practice makes them rivals of traditional faiths. The difference between revolutionary faiths and traditional systems of salvation is basically one of degree. It is not necessary to define exactly where the line is to be drawn between religions and political absolutisms. The real point here is that secular faiths and religious traditions belong together in this analysis, not in the sense of being parallel but in the sense of being rivals. This rivalry constitutes one of the major aspects of the problem of tolerance.

The separation of church and state is generally believed to have emancipated religion; actually, it emancipated the state from holding to any particular traditional religion. This separation was based upon a compromise, arising from the conceptions of life and of man characteristic of the age in which this development occurred, namely, the dualism of body and soul, between spiritual and temporal, between salvation and morality, between reason and revelation, between this world and the hereafter. By means of a division of labor, the state was to take care of all earthly matters, civil, administrative, political, and economic affairs. The worldly state was, in other words, to be in charge of so-called secular matters. The church was to provide for the so-called spiritual salvation of individuals and for the preservation of their souls in the hereafter.[1] This arrangement set up in effect two sovereignties, the sovereignty of the state and the sovereignty of God.

As interest in this-worldly salvation began to take shape, the state quite unconsciously made itself responsible for the salvation of its citizens and thus became a serious competitor of the church.[2] The early formulations of this-worldly salvation were rather vague but nevertheless real. If salvation means the fulfillment of those needs of the individual which require fulfillment in order that life may be deemed worth while, the state was prepared to fulfill those needs in achieving liberty, equality, and fraternity, or, translated into more traditional terms, freedom, justice, and peace.

The existence of two sovereignties did not constitute a problem so long as the jurisdiction of one did not appear to encroach on that of the other. But soon it became clear that the dualism was itself baseless in fact. So-called spiritual qualities very often have their roots in temporal conditions. The souls of men are deeply affected by their physical well-being. Poverty and disease create bitterness, envy, and hatred. Wealth and power often tend to make people callous and heartless. Thus, even those who continued to believe that salvation lay in the hereafter, and who based the qualifications for admittance into the world-to-come upon good behavior in this world, conceded that behavior in this world was very much conditioned by temporal situations.

When the growing mechanization of life brought with it the intensification of such social evils as poverty and vice, "religious leaders" would not consent to confine their activities to the salvation of souls. They became interested in physical well-being too. When this happened, the two sovereignties began to clash.[3]

In the meantime, new faiths[4] began to grow up, offering salvation and a way of life on the basis of a system of beliefs and practices completely alien to the traditions of Christendom or Judaism. These faiths were so insistent, however, upon their rejection of the old civilizations, and even the new civilizations of the modern states, that they became identified with "irreligion"; one of them, communism, considered itself definitely antireligious. Nevertheless, these faiths bore all the identifying marks of religious faiths, particularly the tendency to develop sancta.[5]

Every religious group, in order to insure its unity and coherence in the face of challenge, consecrates whatever in its experience helps to point up the essentials in the system of salvation which that group offers. These are known as sancta; in them the group values are enshrined.

In Christianity, Christmas, the personality of Jesus, Nazareth, Bethlehem, Easter, the Cross, the Bible are sancta. In the United States, the Fourth of July, George Washington, Abraham Lincoln, the Gettysburg cemetery, the Tomb of the Unknown Soldier, the Liberty Bell, though not literally, are at least potentially, sancta, and in time of danger are treated as symbols of something sacred. The symbols of communism are likewise sanctified in and by conflict and challenge.

Thus all faiths, religious or secular, use their sancta to fortify belief in and devotion to the system of salvation which they represent. The interesting fact about sancta is that they are not necessarily dedicated to any fixed system of ethics. Sometimes unconsciously and sometimes deliberately the same sancta are utilized to represent different ethical standards and criteria. In one age slavery is justified in the light of the Bible, and in another age it is condemned in the light of the same sacred book. In one age, the personality of Jesus is invoked in defense of the idea of resignation to evil, and in another age it is invoked as a spur to reform and social militancy. Because of the wide range of possible interpretations, we are likely to find varieties of ethical criteria within any single religious group and to see them invoked in the name of the same sancta. On the other hand, we are as likely to discover that members of two or more groups having common ideals but associating them with different sancta.

In studying the relations between religious groups it is always necessary to distinguish between sancta and ethics because frequently what appears to be a conflict in ethics turns out to be merely reference to a different set of sancta for the same ethics, and vice versa. It must be noted, however, that this analysis of the relation of sancta and ethics is not universally applicable, because there are religious groups that dissociate ethics from salvation. Those systems that regard salvation as a divine mystery attainable through the theurgic power contained in ritual practice do not conceive of their sancta merely as symbolic, or representative. They regard their sancta as inherently potent. When that is the case, sancta are related to salvation directly, and are not, as in the case of other groups, merely symbolic.

Since we are concerned with equity between religious groups, it is well to point out here that the problems of tolerance are particularly complicated by the fact that they are involved with sancta. We might suppose that a religious group would command a greater degree of respect for its views by virtue of the fact that its members identify their program of life with the things that they regard as sacred. When people are known to be following a certain program because they believe that life and death are involved, they are likely to cause others to give long and serious consideration to that program before cavalierly rejecting it or advocating its abolition. It would seem therefore as if religious groups might treat one another with a great deal of respect.

This, however, is not necessarily the case because of the very tendency to confuse sancta and ethics. When criticism of one group is offered by another, the criticism is sometimes launched against the sancta instead of what the sancta stand for. Religionists are generally very sensitive about sancta, and immediately reject any idea which does not agree with that identified with the sancta. On the other hand, people with unscrupulous intent sometimes conceal their purpose behind the cloak of sancta and confuse relations between groups by exploiting the respect in which those who cherish sancta are held. Furthermore, after a period of time during which sancta are exploited for unworthy purposes, religionists are likely to be distrusted in advance as soon as they speak in the name of religion.

But relations between religious groups are complicated by other factors. The presence of sancta is not the only characteristic which renders the problem of religious tolerance more difficult than and, in a real sense, different from the problem of tolerance in other types of relation. Religious groups offer salvation to their adherents, and, insofar as they attempt to extend the scope of their influence and the numbers of their adherents, they seek to offer salvation to others, as well. Each religious group, therefore, regards its work as altruistic. Now the human mind is so constituted that the rejection of an altruistic offer generates more resentment in the one who makes the offer than would resistance to an obviously aggressive act. Competition among those who wish to be of help to others is often fiercer than competition between those who seek something for themselves.

To impute base motives in religious relations is a more dangerous and more explosive procedure than it is in other types of relations. Business people will say of their rivals' methods: "Business is business," and will understand ulterior motives. In politics, too, standards are not generally expected to be higher than necessary. But in religion the slightest intimation that the desire to "save" people is involved with other, less worthy desires is not only bitterly resented but, if uttered by members of one group against another, is likely to destroy for a long time the possibility of a friendly relation.

A fourth factor is present in inter-faith relations which adds to their special quality. The historic religions represent the oldest living and functioning traditions in the western world. Judaism, for example, is the heir of a culture three thousand years old, with a continuous and unbroken history. Christianity reaches back to two thousand years ago; and although the Protestant tradition is only a few hundred years old, it is as old as, or older than, any secular tradition in America. Their very age gives religious groups a feeling that they are entitled to respect and reverence such as are not accorded to newer phenomena, and they are therefore more sensitive than other groups to offense and to insult. Irrespective of worth, old people and old traditions demand and expect special treatment.

Contemporary faiths are thus to be studied, in their interrelations, in the light of these considerations.

In the chapters that follow, we shall discuss various aspects of the problem of religious tolerance: (1) *Religion and public education;* (2) *Religions with foreign homelands;* (3) *Secular faiths in conflict;* and (4) *Relations between various religious groups:* this subsection will include (a) Catholics and Jews versus Protestants; (b) Protestants and Jews versus Catholics; (c) Catholics and Protestants versus Jews; (d) Proselytizing among the various religious groups.

Obviously, no ethical principle can offer a "solution" in the sense of prescribing a practical cure for a precisely stated difficulty. Ethical principles, such as the principle of equity, at best state a problem in such a way as to clarify its implications, to establish a general guide and method for its resolution. The "solutions" offered here may not be the best ones possible; indeed, the principle of equity may be applied far better than it is applied here. One may well ask: Is it not possible for two or more persons to utilize the same principle and arrive at very different, even mutually antagonistic, solutions? If so, the questioner may add, what good is the principle? It does not lead the one who uses it any nearer the best solution than the one who does not utilize that principle? The question may be answered by pointing out that even in the so-called exact sciences, the application by two men of the same scientific principle may lead to two altogether contradictory courses of action.

What has happened? Has the scientific principle broken down? No; an additional factor has been introduced, namely, *judgment,* the human element which makes it possible for two people to view the same situation "objectively", and to arrive at opposite suggestions for future action. If this is true of scientific principles in the realm of the physical sciences, it is certainly true of principles that operate in the realm of ethical and religious values because such principles are not even designed to point a sharp needle to a fine line on a compass.

The discussions that follow, however, are illustrative of the kind of method which a responsible judge might apply to the problems stated, in an effort to utilize the principle of equity. This method is significantly different from the current principles of tolerance.

The methodology here suggested would help a judge or a group of judges to analyze in terms of the polarity between coöperation and individuality cases in which conflicting interests clash. *This is the function of the principle of equity.* If it performs that function, it has justified itself. In applying the principle of equity, it is necessary to state the problem in such a way as to indicate which forces in a conflict represent coöperation and which forces represent individuality. It is then necessary to state clearly how the claims of coöperation and individuality conflict and how they are mutually beneficent. Then a procedure should be sought which would preserve the beneficent polarity while reducing the friction to a minimum. In the issues which are to be discussed, this methodology is used; a critique is offered of the usual analysis of the problems, the values of individuality and coöperation are distinguished, and suggestions are made, on the basis of equity, for the location of the conflicts and of the dangers from these conflicts to both values.

4

RELIGION AND PUBLIC EDUCATION

One of the most widely discussed questions touching upon the relations of the state to religious groups within the state is that of the relations of public education to religious education. For a number of years now, there has been agitation to introduce religion into the public schools.[1] This has come about because of the widespread belief that religion is not being taught, but should be, to the tens of thousands of children who attend the public schools of the United States. According to Brown,

> The exclusion of religion from the public schools (i.e. schools supported by taxation) was due originally not to any opposition to religion, but to the desire on the part of the educators to keep sectarian bickering out of the schools. It was reenforced by the concern of religious groups to avoid control of education by their rivals. The far reaching consequences of the change were not at first realized. . . . The schools have become more consistently secular. . . . (The state) . . . attempts to keep all specifically religious instruction, defined as sectarian instruction, out of tax supported schools.[2]

The question which arises at once is: Are the children indeed being brought up without "religion"? Does not Brown's phrase "described as sectarian instruction" really give a clue to the problem? What the children are not getting, actually, is Christian religion, or Jewish religion. The assumption behind the whole charge that children are being educated without religion is that they are not being taught to believe in Catholicism or Protestantism or Judaism. The need for teaching children to understand the relations of these to each other in their communities is overlooked.

Hence arises the substitute for these particular religions, the cult of the state, a this-worldly system of faith. The religion of patriotism becomes the cultivation of coöperation exclusively, and wins the adherence of citizens not only through the concrete benefits which they derive from identification with "the common faith," but also through the various symbols or sancta associated with it. The American devotee, through his reverence for Washington, Lincoln, the American Flag, the Constitution, the Declaration of Independence, and other American sancta, sees in America not only a means through which he can achieve the fullness of life, but something which school children of any or no (other) religion may in common hold sacred.

Now, from the point of view of our public schools and political community, the religion of patriotism is the coöperation pole in the polarity which characterizes the life of every American man and woman. This coöperation Americans share; this for all is a common faith, bringing within its fold men and women of all races, traditions, ethnic backgrounds, and historic religious associations.[3] In the public schools, when American ideals are taught, when American history is taught, when reverence for great American personalities, outstanding events, epochmaking documents is taught, the children are being taught a religion; they are being offered salvation, and the instrument of that salvation is being presented to them and dramatized for them by means of the sancta of American life and civilization. Even when patriotism is not *a* religion, it includes religious elements—sancta, oaths, loyalty, etc.

It is wrong to say that American children are being brought up without religion; they are being taught a very vital and absorbing religion. In fact, it is recognized as being vital and meaningful to such an extent that those who represent other systems of salvation and other constellations of sancta are frankly worried. They are afraid that this religion of America will so completely absorb the young people that it will smother and destroy all other loyalties. In other words, *"religious" leaders are afraid that the religion which is the result of coöperation may counterbalance loyalty to the religions which represent individuality.* And these fears are well founded. When patriotism becomes too intense, the tendency arises to persecute all those who do not take their patriotism religiously, all those who wish to express their individual faith in terms which are not American in origin or in association. And, after all, Christianity, like Judaism, is a foreign ism. Christianity is associated with Palestine, Nazareth, Bethlehem, a Jew from Asia Minor, a scripture written in Aramaic, later in Greek, later in Latin, later still in "King James" English, lastly in American. When patriotism runs amok, all foreign isms, including Christianism, are persecuted as conflicting faiths. The state becomes completely intolerant of other gods.

If we wish to approach the problem creatively, we must clarify the issues. Taking the political or common faith as the whole, the Christians of a particular denomination X are a part. When Christians X foster their religious individuality they are enriching the common faith,

and when they practice the common faith they enrich their individualities, provided that they engage in both in the spirit of equity. Each
pole may fructify the other. American life has demonstrated on numer-
ous occasions how this reciprocity works. For example, many churches
and synagogues have added a holiday to their calendar on Thanksgiving
Day and Memorial Day. Conversely, American holidays have been
greatly enriched by the introduction of prayers and readings from the
Judeo-Christian tradition. Americanism should be enriched by and
influenced by Christianism and vice versa. Both can be regarded le-
gitimately as religious or sacred institutions, and the citizen would be
understood as belonging to two faiths simultaneously. Where the loyal
citizen has no other faith, intolerance and persecution are likely to follow because the faiths which he is called upon to tolerate are not "lived"
in the same person; what adjustments *are* made are dictated by external requirements, not by inner compatibility. Where both religions
are practiced, there is an inner basis for equity.

If, then, the public school is a training ground in the religion of
America, is there any reason for introducing the teachings of Christianism, of the X variety, into the school? I believe that it has no place
there, though indirectly those who teach Americanism, if they are, outside school, members of the Christian X group, will undoubtedly enrich
the Americanism lesson by virtue of that fact. But the direct teaching
of Christianism X does not belong there, because pedagogical incompatibilities would soon appear as religious conflicts.

It has been suggested by F. Ernest Johnson[4] and others that part of
the problem could be obviated by offering to children in the public
schools an analysis of religion in culture, developing in them "a religious
sensitiveness and appreciation." The public school should "insure that
the minds of children are not left closed to the religious elements in
our cultural heritage. . . . Public education should lead children directly into a sympathetic understanding of religious institutions." These
suggestions still leave the problem of religious education unsolved. This
approach may at best teach children *about* religion, *about* religions and
about the place of religion in their culture, but give no training *in*
religion. It does not follow necessarily that the more we know about
religion and its institutions, the more likely we are to be religious.
Johnson's proposals are well worth considering for their intrinsic merit;
but they are not calculated to desecularize public education.

Is there any objection to released time on the ground that the public
school should not be "implicated" in religious activities? According to

the principle of equity, the pole of coöperation should be "implicated" in the pole of individuality. Just as the good school will encourage individual differences, so it should in equity evoke from the children the expression of their respective individual religions in the environment of public coöperation rather than permit religious differences to live only in an atmosphere of segregation and exclusiveness. Care should, therefore, be taken to protect from discrimination and insult those who express individuality by not having any individuality in religion, and to encourage compatibility in individual differences.

There are some serious objections to released time from the point of view of equity. First, released time may not give sufficient time to those groups which have more to teach than they can get into one hour a week, if they are genuinely to cultivate their individuality. It is a mechanical kind of equality which is practiced when all groups are given one hour a week. What they need is not equality but equity: some religious groups find that in one hour a week they can barely whet the appetite of the child, and then they are forced to leave him frustrated—and the teacher thwarted. Let us assume, for example, that the Christian group X can convey what they regard as the essentials in one hour a week. That should not militate against permitting Jewish group B from having their children four hours a week, if the latter group finds that they do more harm than good by offering one hour of instruction a week. In other words, the balance must be flexible to provide for fluctuating needs. In certain instances it is necessary to emphasize coöperation in order to overcome an exaggerated individuality. When children of a very tender age are just beginning to leave the family circle and to cultivate their public relations, to overemphasize their home individuality is harmful. Thus the process of separating the Catholic children from the Jewish children, from the various groups of Protestant children, *in public* is a process calculated to work harm. The larger coöperation in children is still so poorly developed that the individuality stressed by the public segregation of religious groups may do much harm to the common faith.[5] On the other hand, after school, when the children naturally drift off in the direction of their respective homes and neighborhoods, and their individuality comes naturally to the fore, it is appropriate to send them to their respective religious schools. Now, in equity, the aim should be to adjust the school day so that the children have time to express their individuality without overburdening their program and without affecting their coöperation. A shorter public school day may be needed in some communities to obviate the danger referred to by Dawson:

> What modern Christians have to fear is not the danger of violent persecution but rather that of the crushing out of religion [meaning, of course, a particular religion] from modern life by the sheer weight of a state-inspired public opinion and by the mass organization of society on a purely secular [meaning "religion of patriotism"] basis.

There is no evidence at hand to prove that children who are released an hour earlier will, necessarily, use that hour each day cultivating the unique interests which they share with others of their faith, historic or secular. There is no guarantee that they will not spend that hour in the theater or in outdoor sports, activities which they share with all other Americans. Nevertheless, the cause of equity is advanced if those who do have a religious individuality to express and to fulfill are given an opportunity for its expression and fulfillment by being released early, provided that the hours are not curtailed to a point where the public becomes inadequate. For the public education system to dominate the entire time of children is to violate the principle of equity, since the public system cannot be made responsible for cultivating religious individuality. The amount of time needed for the cultivation of religious individuality may be an hour; it may be ten hours. If the individuality does not express itself in the time granted, at least no injustice will have been done, provided the education of citizens does not suffer.

All that has been said thus far applies to the relations between the state and the Protestants, and the state and the Jews, religious groups whose opinion overwhelmingly favors the public school, in its broadest terms, and whose religious leaders are content to work for the most part with the public school system. The problem as it affects the Catholics is somewhat different. The Catholic Church would consider it most satisfactory if they could supervise the entire education of Catholic children. Catholic leaders do not hesitate to declare that the public schools are a poor substitute for parochial education. Indeed, if there were enough such parochial schools, no Catholic children would be encouraged to attend public schools. Now, in wishing to educate their own children, the Catholics give emphasis to their individuality. Is this emphasis at the expense of coöperation? If so, shall parochial schools be barred? This question has come up many times. In the famous Oregon case, the matter was settled by the Supreme Court, which refused to outlaw parochial schools. We may infer from this opinion of the Supreme Court that this expression of individuality was not inconsistent with the unity and integrity of the state. This is undoubtedly the case. Parochial education need not take the Catholic out of American life. As a matter of fact, Catholics are as active in the civic and communal life of the country as members of any other group. But there is always the danger that parochial schools generate a "parochial" outlook. And the state is equitably concerned in preventing this result.

Since there are not enough parochial schools, many thousands of Catholic children attend the public schools. Catholic educators are naturally concerned about these children, but under present conditions there seems to be no other alternative; they have to be content to permit these children to attend the public schools. They must therefore join with teachers of other faiths who wish to supplement the public school education with "religious" education; and so far as that is concerned, they would certainly favor released time. This is a mere expedient, however, for Catholics, since they do not recognize the desirability of separating religious and secular studies.

If the time should ever come when the Catholic Church sought to remove the greatest number of its children from the public schools, thus withdrawing them from free intercourse with their fellow Americans, or if the Church should find that it could not, for doctrinal reasons, "tolerate" the public school system and the religion of patriotism that it inculcates, the issue would be sharply drawn between individuality and coöperation. In that event, Americans would have to apply the principle of equity with great care. It is always possible, of course, both in theory and practice, that conflicts become so basic that equity is helpless.

A question related to those just discussed has to do with religious and public morals. Religious bodies even when they do not seek to introduce religion into public education directly may seek to exert their influence upon the choice of public educators. They sometimes feel that public instruction under particular teachers may prejudice students against those moral standards with which religions in the contemporary western world have been identified.

A dramatic example is the well-known Bertrand Russell case, which occurred during 1940 in the city of New York. The distinguished philosopher and pedagogue was elected by the Board of Higher Education of the city of New York to teach mathematics and logic. Church leaders organized a movement to prevent his teaching at the College of the City of New York, to which he had been appointed. The movement gathered considerable momentum, and finally the immediate issue was resolved in a way that left the essential problem unsolved: the professorship was dropped from the budget. But the question continued to agitate people. Had the church leaders the right to interfere in the affairs of the college of the city? Should not the church confine itself to "religion"? Was not the principle of academic freedom violated?

Invoking the principle of academic freedom confused the issue in the minds of many people. Certainly, teachers should have the freedom to teach what they believe about what they are supposed to teach, and should not be dictated to—and yet there is obviously another side to the question. Have not the "religious" citizens in a community the right to check upon the teachers who influence the children? Has not the community freedom to refuse to employ a teacher? If the professor insists upon academic freedom, the community may also insist upon *its* freedom.[6] Without raising the other issues of freedom, we must ask here: How far can "private" religions go equitably in influencing "public" morals?

Those who claimed that the church should not be interested in the morals of a public teacher found themselves unable to square that view with the view that religion ought to be a force for social good and should concern itself with public morals. Those on the side of the teacher insisted that they were for "freedom", and those who opposed the teacher claimed that they were opposed to "license." In the end, those who shouted loudest and lobbied longest had their way. But the ethical problem, the equitable criterion of action, remains unarticulated.[7]

The whole incident might have been more fruitful of valuable discussion and more satisfactorily resolved for all the parties concerned if the question had not been approached from either one or the other pole in the situation, but from both. The pole of individuality represented by Russell and his colleagues offered some admitted and common values: the search for truth unimpeded, the right of the individual conscience, the independence of public officials from partisan pressure interfering in academic administration. These values are in the interests of individuality. On the other hand, the pole of coöperation had its recognized values to offer: the morals of the community, the religious sensibilities of its citizens, the common responsibility of all public officials to the will and morals of the community.

An attempt to establish an equilibrium between the poles in such a way as to satisfy the demands of each on the basis of the principle of equity, and an open and honest declaration to the effect that such an attempt was being made, would have been more conducive to the advancement of the values represented by both than was the procedure adopted, even the court procedure, which was not based on equity in this sense. What would the principle of equity have suggested? From the point of view of equity Russell would necessarily have had to prove in some way that he acknowledged his responsibilities to a community, a majority of whose members seemed to object to his presence on the faculty of a tax-supported institution. On the other hand, the cause of equity might have been spared a defeat if the Board of Higher Education had officially raised relevant issues of professional ethics. One of the requirements of a teacher in a public institution should be his avowed respect for the moral code of his community and refusal to exploit his public office for extraneous ends. Any candidate for a position in a public school should have to pass an appropriate character test. Such a test by the responsible officials might have prevented irresponsible tests by unresponsible bodies. Though religious bodies obviously have moral interests they should not assume that they are the "guardians" of public morals.

It is equitable that any one with a message to deliver to the young of the city should know under what conditions he will be permitted to deliver that message. In addition to his academic requirements, he should have to measure up to certain moral requirements. If he believes sufficiently in his message and if his message conflicts with the requirements of his public office, he ought to be content to express his individual differences in a private capacity, in a school privately subsidized by those who are willing to support him. So long as the system of voluntary association prevails, and so long as private groups may establish schools, such teachers will not be altogether deprived of individuality. It is not, however, the function of public schools to promote the very opposite of coöperation.

The question arises: What if the "moral requirements" were made to include abstention from smoking, drinking, and gambling? Religious groups in various parts of the country object to some or all of these practices. Could they not make a character committee reject any teachers who indulged in any of these "vices"? If the religious groups in a community were strong enough and influential enough, and those who disagreed were not interested enough to make their opinions heard, the character committee might certainly be inclined to include these practices in their list of criteria, on the assumption that the religious groups were typical of the community as a whole. The fact that Russell smokes a pipe never came up in the New York situation for precisely the reason that the public sentiment against smoking was infinitesimal. But if the community considered smoking in the same category with adultery, it would have been justified in raising the question.

In any event, unless some machinery is set up which cultivates equity, every time such an issue arises, each pole will clamor for exclusive recognition.

5

RELIGIONS WITH FOREIGN HOMELANDS

We have looked into two aspects of the relation of the state and religious groups within the state, one touching upon the introduction of religion into public education and the other upon the attempt by religious groups to influence the choice of teachers in the public schools. We have seen that in the light of the principle of equity the moral and religious issues have been clarified. We shall now explore the relation of the state to religious groups that associate their religion with a foreign geographical area. In discussing such groups, the purpose is to clarify the question of "dual loyalties," a charge brought against a number of religious groups whose religious traditions go back to foreign lands, or whose churches are still associated with religious homelands elsewhere. The question, to be sure, is not one in which only the state is involved, in relation to such groups. Very often, in inter-religious relations, members of religious groups raise questions about members of other religious groups and seek to call the attention of the authorities to what they regard as dangerous situations. For example, some Jews question the "patriotism" of Catholics, while some Catholics question the "patriotism" of some Zionist Jews, and Protestants frequently raise questions about both Catholics and Jews. Though each religious group appears to be coming to the defense of the state, there are religious issues underlying the political. These we shall discuss later.

Religious groups with foreign homelands are not exemplified by the Catholics and Jews alone. For instance, the Greek-Orthodox Church has a very close sense of kinship with the Greek state. On March 24, 1941, the Greeks in the city of New York celebrated the 120th anniversary of Hellenic independence, and ten thousand Greek-Americans in picturesque native costumes marched in parade with banners flying. The celebration reached it climax with special religious services conducted by Archbishop Athenagoras of the Greek-Orthodox Church.[1] The annual celebration of St. Patrick's Day is another familiar example of a tie-up between an American religious group and a territorial entity on foreign soil. It is mentioned here because it represents a complicated pattern: it is Catholic, Irish, and American, as distinguished from some other Catholic groups which are not involved with a national as well as with a church homeland.

To what extent shall such religious groups be permitted to teach their children a love for and a sense of kinship with a land to which they are not native but which constitutes the homeland of the religious culture which they practice? Is there not a political involvement here which spells dual loyalty of an objectionable kind? In other words, how far shall a state tolerate not only the cultural pluralism which this creates but the actual self-identification on the part of thousands of men and women with another country.

These questions are part of a larger issue, to be sure. The relations between the citizens of the United States and the political fortunes of other nations have been very liberal. American citizens are permitted to volunteer to fight in the armies of foreign countries, provided, of course, that those countries are not at war with the United States. If that is true in times of war, why should it not be equally true in times of peace? Why, in other words, should not a Greek in America wish to consider himself still a Greek by nationality, and even a Greek patriot, so long as loyalty to Greece does not in any way interfere with his patriotism as an American? Particularly if he continues to identify himself with Greece through Greco-American fraternal, social, and religious organizations, the danger of political disloyalty is reduced to a minimum.

The group most vitally involved in this matter are the Roman Catholics. It is a familiar fact that the Vatican maintains all the outward appurtenances of a political state, but the Catholic Archbishop Spellman, in a statement by an authoritative spokesman of the Church, stressed the fact that the Vatican is a state.[2] Archbishop Spellman in discussing President Roosevelt's appointment of Myron C. Taylor as representative to the Vatican for the purpose of pursuing peace in Europe, said:

> The Holy Father is not alone the supreme head of the Catholic Church. He is also head of a sovereign State. Thirty-eight countries have representatives at the Holy See. Nobody protests because President Roosevelt has an Ambassador to Great Britain, even though King George VI is the head of the Church of England. The heads of other countries are also heads of religions in those countries. . . .

It appears that from Archbishop Spellman's point of view the Pope is head of a State; and also the head of a Church.

Both the size of the Roman Catholic population in the United States and the intensiveness of its program have made non-Catholic Americans particularly suspicious of Catholics. The representative of the overwhelming number of Americans, namely, the Protestant,

> senses in the imposing edifice of the Catholic Church essentially a
> superstate which, however much it may seek to distinguish between
> the temporal and the spiritual, is actually always confusing the two.
> . . . He therefore sees in Roman Catholicism a bid for universal
> power, founded on the wreckage of the Roman Empire and bearing
> countless evidences of its Italian origin in its spiritual imperial-
> ism. . . .[3]

He bases his suspicion on the political character of the Church but also specifically upon individual instances of attempts to place the authority of the Vatican above that of the states in which Catholics reside.

The National Conference of Christians and Jews smooths over the whole question with a statement minimizing the possibility of conflict. Discussing the charge against the Catholics that "the relation of Catholics to the Pope in Rome [is] regarded as involving a divided political allegiance," the Conference suggests the following answer:

> The proof of the pudding, reasonable men will agree, is in the eat-
> ing. In more than 150 years of national existence there has been no
> example of conflict between the allegiances that American Catholics
> owe to the United States and that which they owe to the Pope. Never-
> theless, American Catholics should take every opportunity to make
> clear to their fellow citizens of other faiths the spiritual nature of
> their allegiance to the Vatican.[4]

The probability is that no instance of "conflict" arose because the American people have seldom elected a Catholic to a position of responsibility in the government where he might be in a position to face such a conflict. But aside from this point, to talk of the "spiritual nature" of Catholics' relation to the Vatican in one case and to insist upon the "political" character of the Vatican in another case is obviously shifting positions for convenience. When it is convenient to protest loyalty to the United States, the Holy See becomes purely "spiritual"; when it is convenient to establish the propriety of sending ambassadors and representatives to the Vatican, it becomes "political."

No, the Roman Catholic Church stands in the same relation to the Catholic citizens of the United States as that of the Greek-Orthodox

Church to Greek-Americans; and as that of the Anglican Church to Anglican-Americans. They are all in the same category; they represent religious authority thoroughly involved with temporal sovereignty. It might be argued that the United States should treat them all alike, and that the only question is: should they all be tolerated, or should none, and on what basis?

Each case should be studied individually; if equity is to prevail, we must analyze the relation which each group bears to its homeland, and to the United States, and then attempt to arrive at a condition in which both poles would be compatible. We must first, therefore, articulate the common values which each of the poles seeks to preserve and advance. We should point, for example, to the need of religious groups to draw spiritual sustenance from the sancta of their unique civilizations. In order to live in the light of a religion's teachings, and to find self-fulfillment in them, people must be free to identify their ethical strivings with personalities, events, objects, and places which constitute the sacred associations of their group and the significant experiences in its history. If, however, that set of sancta happen to occupy, in space, positions outside the geographical unit in which the members of the religious group find themselves, consideration has to be given to that geographical community which, according to our analysis, represents the pole of coöperation—the state—for in that community a particular church is but a part.

The state seeks its own welfare and that of all its citizens. We should see to it that its claims, legitimate and compelling, are clearly stated, and that its fears are set forth with proper sympathy. When the values of both have been carefully studied, the resolution of many difficulties is bound to result. But certainly no good can come from the exclusive reiteration of one principle, that of patriotism, or of the other, that of religious freedom. The former sees only evil in "dual loyalties"; it sees no evil in a purely monistic culture. The latter sees value in universalism, but neglects the dangers of "fifth column" treason in the guise of religious devotion. Whether we are dealing with Catholics, Jews, or Greek-Orthodox, the principle of equity can be effectively applied. With every desire in the world to enrich American life with the religious (and ethnic) contributions of all nations, the United States would be compelled to lean toward a very stringent homogeneity, in the interests of coöperation, if a legitimate fear arose that foreign elements were proving too dangerous. On the other hand, if no such danger existed, the most sincere desire to safeguard American civilization would not be sufficient reason for discouraging the cultivation of foreign ethnic and religious cultures.

These commonplaces are repeated here not as solutions of the problem, but as evidence that the problem is one of equilibrium. Neither state nor church under these conditions can claim absolute freedom; nor is the optimism realistic that assumes that spiritual and temporal loyalties are by nature not incompatible. The tension between these loyalties is real and the problem is one of giving due or equitable weight (according to changing circumstances) to both factors. Unilateral claims merely confuse the moral issues.

6

SECULAR FAITHS IN CONFLICT

An important area of religious conflict exists in the relationships between secular faiths. Secular faiths, as they have been described, are those competing, militant systems of salvation represented by modern politico-economic-social theories and loyalties, among which are democracy, fascism-Nazism, and communism. They are secular in the sense that they have a political embodiment. They are religious in that they include a cosmic orientation and faith, an ethics, and a complex of ritual, symbolism, and sancta, which hallow them.

The conflict that arises is in a true sense a religious conflict. And the problem of tolerance that grows out of that conflict is a problem in religious tolerance. Specifically, the question of tolerance arises when defenders of democracy ask whether the proponents of opposing systems should be entitled to make use of the rights which democracy provides in order to destroy it. Freedom of speech, assembly, and the press are invoked as rights by Nazis and communists to defend their own right to advocate a change in the order of things. So far, no one has been able to discover one occasion when they have invoked the freedom of religion—which, to be sure, is the right most relevant to the question. Those who believe that individuality is of paramount importance would do nothing to curtail the "freedom" of individuals or of groups within the nation. A spokesman for this view is Frank Murphy:[1]

> You do not and cannot strengthen or protect democracy by undermining it. And you begin to undermine democracy the moment you begin to draw the line and say that this or that person shall not have civil liberty. Draw the line against one group and it is an easy step to draw it against another and then another.

Murphy rests upon a concept of the late Oliver Wendell Holmes, "free trade in ideas", and he adds:

> Simply stated, that concept means that democracy gives a hearing to every idea. It gives every philosophy the opportunity to get itself accepted in the competition of the market. And ultimately, as our history shows, the true idea, the right policy comes out on top.

It is interesting to observe that Justice Murphy, in attempting to justify a course of action based upon only one pole, namely, individuality, instead of upon the two poles, of individuality and coöperation, falls into a number of fallacies which he would otherwise certainly have avoided. First, the doctrine that the right policy always comes out on top does not stand up under careful scrutiny. Cohen has characterized that belief as resting

> on a peculiar dullness to the pathetic and tragic elements in history, such, for instance, as the crushing of several types of civilization. . . . Like other forms of brutality, this glorification of the historically actual is due to a lack of sympathy or imagination which prevents us from seeing all the finer possibilities, hopes and aspirations, at the expense of which the triumph of the actual is frequently purchased. The doctrine that right always triumphs is but an insidious form of the immoral doctrine that what triumphs (i.e. might) is always right.[2]

Another fallacy which Murphy falls into is that of applying the principle of "free trade in ideas" to the problem of granting civil liberties to those who oppose free trade in ideas. The Nazis and the communists do not offer their ideas honestly in the market place. They do what many merchants do: they disguise their commodities. They dress them up. They put them in attractive bottles. They offer them to the public under names which are misleading. A pure food and drug act had to be passed in order to expose to the light the exact ingredients of the commodities offered by merchants. There is no pure idea act. If there were, free trade in ideas might work better than it does.[3]

As a result of the absence of such a law, and the tendencies of "subversive" groups, Nazism and communism are offered to the lovers of democracy *as democracy*. In fact, the new faiths are described as being the only true democracy; the so-called "democracies" now operating are called misleading and enslaving, false and counterfeit. The new faiths are described as reflecting the true will of the people. Gaetano Salvemini writes:

> The Fascists, the Nazis, and the Communists also often and readily dub as "democracy", nay more, as the "real", "true", "full", "substantial", "more honest" democracy the political regimes of present-day Italy, Germany and Russia, because these regimes . . . profess to comfort and uplift lower classes after having deprived them of the

very political rights without which it is not possible to conceive of "government by the people."[4]

The advocates of fascism-Nazism and communism, like the merchants, in order to develop good will toward their offerings, bring about, in the minds of the public, series of pleasant associations with those offerings which are extraneous to their inherent and essential worth. They package their programs of action in sancta which are accepted by Americans and then attempt to effect a transfer of affection and loyalty from the sancta to the program. Not only do they label their system "democracy"; they exploit the heroes of American democracy for their purpose. For example, when isolation happens to fit in with the communist program of the moment, the communists exploit the cherished name of George Washington and the sacred associations of the famous Farewell Address to impress upon Americans the need for isolation, but when "collective security" is the prevailing philosophy they invoke the memory of Woodrow Wilson and his ideal of international coöperation. The Nazis glorify the names of famous German Americans like Carl Schurz, not to advance the cause which they represented but to develop associations of good will with personalities of German origin and thus to stimulate good will toward Germany itself.

These tactics are undoubtedly known to Murphy; yet he ignores them because he cannot accommodate himself to the thought that civil liberties merely constitute one pole in the individuality-coöperation polarity. In the same way, Murphy permits himself to say that when the line is drawn against one group, "it is an easy step to draw it against another, and then another," as a defense of not drawing it at all. Obviously, some restrictions always exist in a society. Men are not absolutely free to say anything and everything. Incitement to violence is forbidden, and punishable. Is that not "drawing the line" somewhere? Why should that not also be frowned upon on the ground that it might lead to drawing the line "against another and then another"? The fact is, as Bertrand Russell has stated it, that when we are confronted with a group

fundamentally opposed to a governmental theory accepted by the majority, and . . . violence is intended to be used at a suitable moment, there is every justification for preventing the growth of organized power in the hands of a rebellious minority. For if this is not done internal peace is jeopardized, and the kind of community that most men desire can no longer be preserved. Liberal principles will not survive of themselves; like all other principles, they require vigorous assertion when they are challenged.[5]

In other words, Nazism or communism is actually inciting to intolerance, although the spokesman at a particular moment may be invoking tolerance as a sacred right.

Russell has thus spoken up for coöperation. In the interests of "internal peace," he is quite prepared to muzzle the enemies of tolerance. But he does not go far enough in his discussion to formulate a criterion. He asks the pertinent and vital questions clearly enough:

> Does the principle of free speech require us to put no obstacle in the way of those who advocate its suppression? Does the principle of toleration require us to tolerate those who advocate intolerance? Public opinion among those who dislike fascism is divided on these questions, and has not arrived at any clear theory from which consistent answers could be derived.[6]

Apparently, it is not "public opinion" alone that "has not arrived at any clear theory." Reinhold Niebuhr, who also champions coöperation, says: "In a given instance, the principle of freedom may have to yield to the necessities of social cohesion, requiring a measure of coercion. . . . [But] on the question of the relative value of freedom and solidarity, no final and authoritative answer can be given. . . ."[7] We do not expect a final answer but we do expect some answer, and none is forthcoming from Mr. Niebuhr. He asserts that the answer depends upon the individual solutions. Granted; but I believe that the problem in the various situations can be approached from the point of view of a principle which would apply to all.

Herbert W. Schneider, in his essay "The Liberties of Man," summarizing all the papers contained in the volume *Freedom: Its Meaning*, describes the same failure to arrive at a clear theory. He tells us that

> MacIver at least states the problem very clearly: "What combination of liberties and restraints is most serviceable for the existence of what men seek when they place a high value on liberty?" He continues: "but our immediate concern is with . . ." something else. This, alas, is the sad history of our problem. [The difficulties of the problem might perhaps account for these failures.] To prescribe the conditions under which conscience can breathe freely is an exceedingly delicate task, for liberty complains of suffocation the moment you touch her. It is usually a technical problem rather than a moral one, if we may make so dubious a distinction.

I contend that the distinction is a real distinction but that the problem is both a moral and a technical one. The criterion which Russell is seeking, and which should govern any approach to a resolution of conflicts, is the principle of equity: *Make for individuality so long as it enhances coöperation, and vice versa.* This is the moral standard which should apply to all the various situations. Technically, the problem must be approached by experts dealing with each situation individually.

This means concretely that in a democracy the secular faiths of Nazism and communism must on principle be allowed freedom of expression, and that this freedom of expression must be curtailed—also on principle—when the unity and integrity of the nation appear to be in danger. The same criterion that provides for freedom of speech, press, and assembly for the enemies of democracy provides for restriction, when restriction is necessary to re-establish the proper equilibrium. From this point of view, Murphy's position is rejected because it rests only upon individuality, while the positions suggested by Russell, Niebuhr, and MacIver are regarded as inadequate because they do not state their philosophic bases.

They seem to make their recommendations to curtail freedom in despair of ever following through a theory to its logical conclusion. It is as though they say: "Freedom is the desideratum; but freedom is only theoretically a good thing. If you try to apply freedom, you find that practically it won't work. In some situations you must simply abandon theory and recognize realities." As was pointed out above, Perry says the same thing in substance. Such an attitude toward the theory of freedom is not necessary, if the theory is correct. There is no need for apologies when individuality is curtailed, if this is done in the process of applying the principle of equity. Only MacIver appears to recognize that liberties and restraints are coördinates, though he makes "restraints" appear to be of a negative character. Actually, the pole opposite liberty is positive, representing the values of coöperation. But in any case he approaches the matter purely as a technical problem. We must repeat: it is not just a technical problem. Indeed, no problem can be thoroughly understood without an appreciation of the values with which it is involved and the generalizations of which it is an instance. The principle of equity provides that generalization in the problem of religious tolerance.

In applying the principle of equity to the problem of extending religious freedom to those who do not believe in it for others, we should take into consideration the various factors that distinguish this type of conflict from others which are not of a religious character. For example, as has been suggested, the sincerity of the proponents of a secular faith should be taken into consideration. When a group identify their philosophy and program with everything that they regard as sacred, even though the sancta of that group are different from the sancta of the majority and hence bear no sanctity for the majority—that group must be taken more seriously than another whose members are not dedicated to their task to the same extent. More respect is due a group of men and women who are prepared to suffer, and even to die, for a cause, a way of life, a system of salvation, than is due a group whose demands seem to be motivated by more superficial interests.

Sometimes a deeply felt conviction is not relatable to any sancta, popularly recognized as such. For example, conscientious objectors who take their stand in the name of a well-known religious teacher are acknowledged to be conscientious. If the teacher is obscure, and not listed among the generally accepted religious teachers, it is necessary to avoid dismissing these objectors, in his name, with the casual criticism that the objection is not "conscientious".

At the same time, it would be necessary to be doubly careful not to be tricked into acting unwisely because of the very reasoning described. Unscrupulous individuals utilize the sancta of religion in order to earn a degree of consideration which they know they would not otherwise receive. The technical problem lies in distinguishing when conscience is really suffocating, and when it is only pretending to—and when, as a matter of fact, conscience is involved at all. Certainly, Schneider points out elsewhere, people should be free to speak according to their conscience, but it is necessary to analyze the "speeches to find out how many of them are conscientious."[8]

Democracy as a secular faith, as a system of this-worldly salvation, finds its existence greatly jeopardized by rival secular faiths, and simultaneously by its very effort to ward off their attack. Measures are bound to be introduced which will sacrifice individuality to coöperation in the immediate future, and for some time to come. If the American people want democracy not to perish from the earth, they must keep alive their loyalty not only to their country but to the individualities of all those individuals and groups within the country that represent the pole of individuality. No matter how long it takes to restore the normal balance, that balance must be restored, and equity re-established.

RELATIONS BETWEEN RELIGIOUS GROUPS

We have been considering the relation of religious groups to the state insofar as public education is concerned, the relation to the state of religious groups which have foreign homelands, and the relation of the secular faiths to the state. Throughout I have emphasized those cases where the state itself represents a secular faith, being something sacred to its adherents. For that reason we may say that in a true sense we have been discussing inter-faith relations. But in the popular mind "inter-faith relations" deal exclusively with the relations existing between the various traditional religious groups.

The relations between historic religious groups do constitute, if not the exclusive content, at least a considerable part of the content of inter-faith relations. The problem of religious tolerance cannot be said to have been studied thoroughly until careful consideration has been given to the causes of tension between the various groups which form parts of the whole American community and which fall into the traditional categories of Catholic, Protestant, and Jewish. Our theoretical problem is complicated here by the difficulty of finding a pole of coöperation inherent in interreligious relations.

A. CATHOLICS AND JEWS VS. PROTESTANTS

In analyzing the conflicts that exist among the Protestant-Catholic-Jewish groups, our best guide is the outline found in *The American Way*,[1] prepared by the National Conference of Christians and Jews. According to that outline, "Non-Protestants list the following causes of tension between groups, for which Protestants are said to be responsible: 1. The close alliance of Protestantism with the political theories of "nationalism" which in its militant form is the main foe of religion in the contemporary world. . . . 2. The failure of Protestants adequately to cast their weight against persecution of Catholics in Mexico and Jews in Germany. . . . 3. Discrimination against Catholics and Jews in school jobs, public works, and elsewhere. . . . 4. Confusion of bigotry and narrowness with religious earnestness. . . . 5. Discrimination in Sunday School literature, especially in connection with the crucifixion story, of interpretations of history prejudicial to the Jews. . . ." Thus far the charges against the Protestants.

1. *Protestantism and Nationalism:* This problem should be stated more clearly. The real problem is the relation of the modern national state, functioning as a faith, to the historic religious groups. I have attempted in an earlier chapter to investigate this relation. As presented in the outline, the Protestants are held responsible for helping the religion of the state to supplant the historic religions. Thus the conflict between the Protestants and other groups is, in this instance, merely another phase of the problem of the secular faith of the modern nation versus the historic faiths. To say, however, that "nationalism" is the foe of "religion" is only to confuse matters;[2] and unfortunately that confusion is characteristic of most good-will advocates, who use the term "religion" only in association with the historic religions.

2. *Failure to oppose persecution:* This charge against the Protestants was made in 1935. Obviously, the particular situation to which it refers is somewhat changed at the present time (1941); yet the fundamental issue remains. The Catholics and the Jews were impatient with the indifference shown by Protestants toward the suppression of Jews in Germany and of Catholics in Mexico. Protestants should have realized that when coöperation completely dominates, and individuality is thoroughly suppressed, Protestantism itself is bound to be jeopardized sooner or later. This charge relates to the problem of the state versus religious groups within the state, and to the indirect assistance which the Protestants were giving the state in its program of crushing individuality. Thus, this charge is really a phase of the first.

3. *Discrimination in jobs:* This is, of course, a serious charge, but it has little to do with religious tolerance directly. Rarely do Catholics and Jews suffer discrimination because of their religious views. Discrimination in the economic realm is involved with social prejudices and false generalizations regarding members of certain racial, ethnic, and national groups. If religious questions enter at all, they enter as vestiges of long standing feuds which, generally speaking, have no relevance at the present time. Of course, there are people who are convinced that Judaism teaches its adherents to rob and cheat and who would naturally refuse to engage the services of a pious Jew who took his religion seriously. But since discrimination against Jews includes the Jews who are utterly indifferent to their religion, this consideration loses all its value.

4. *Confusing bigotry with earnestness:* The point at which devotion becomes bigotry, and religious earnestness becomes narrowness, depends upon the attitude of the observer. The identical manifestations of re-

ligious fervor may appear to the sympathetic person as deep piety and to the unsympathetic as viciousness. Therefore the charge made against Protestants, that they accuse others of bigotry, is merely another way of saying that Protestants are unsympathetic toward the sancta or the ethics of other groups. Now, we have observed before that in all disagreements it is usually most helpful to clarify the issues. Name calling does not help. To ask Protestants to stop calling names should seem superfluous, but it is apparently necessary.

From the term "bigoted" it is an easy step to the word "superstitious." After that, it is very easy to discredit a religion altogether. The principle of equity depends to a great extent upon the careful distinction between ethics and sancta, or, in other words, between what a religious group offers as its program and the names in which that program is offered. The sanctity of the name—or the place, the event, the institution, the book—is nontransferable; that name is not sacred, in fact, it means absolutely nothing, to members of another religious group. For another religious group to label the sancta "superstitions" is to violate not only good taste but equity. On the other hand, if the opposition applies to the ethics, then certainly name calling does not advance the cause of equity. A system of ethics must be judged by its purpose and by the extent to which it can achieve that purpose. If Protestants and Jews disagree with certain aspects of the Catholic program, they should stick to the point and discuss only the program—not the sacred doctrine, or personality, in whose name that program has been promulgated.

5. *The crucifixion story:* Freedom to teach Christianity must exclude the freedom to incite to violence or to discrimination, in accordance with the implications of the principle of equity thus far evolved. If Protestants insist that they cannot tell the story of the crucifixion without implicating contemporary Jews in the "guilt," they must be charged with inciting to both. Freedom to teach Christianity must include the freedom to articulate and to communicate those positive values which characterize Christian religion and ethics. These values can undoubtedly be taught without the accompanying incitement to hate. Many Protestants already understand how well that can be done, and they have done it. Others must certainly follow suit if the principle of equity is to function.

The National Conference of Christians and Jews finds that when anti-Jewish interpretations of the crucifixion story have "been called to the attention of those responsible for such teaching, where it occurs, it has been gladly remedied." It would be a fine thing if the sanguine report of the Conference were entirely correct. But the question arises: Suppose that Protestants were to invoke their right to "religious freedom" in defense of their right to teach that the Jews living today are guilty of killing Christ?

The principle of equity would demand that such teaching be regarded as an aspect of individuality; and if it could be shown, as I believe it could, that this teaching did result in the practice of discrimination, that individuality would have to be curtailed in the interests of coöperation. In matters of this sort, merely "calling" to people's "attention" is not enough. Legal prescription is necessary. To be sure, care must be taken to avoid the abuse of any laws relating to group libel. Many difficulties stand in the way of proper administration of such laws.

But we should not for that reason reject the principle that religious groups within a state must not be permitted to treat the members of other religious groups in such a way as to jeopardize the security of the latter and the unity of the whole. Nor must we reject the idea that the violation of this principle should be punishable by law. This idea was indeed rejected by a Jewish group, the American Jewish Committee. An advisory committee of lawyers, of the American Jewish Committee, brought in a report discouraging the use of legislation to punish libelous statements against the Jews, their "paramount" objection being that action might be taken which would "violate the constitutional guarantees of freedom of speech, of the press, and of assembly." "In such cases," the statement concluded, "it may be the part of wisdom to adopt other means of defending the civil rights of Jews, principally, a long-range program of education against the deep-rooted, but not insoluble, prejudice."[3]

Thus the principle of equity was overlooked. By seeing the problem only from the one pole of individuality, these Jews hesitated in the name of "freedom" to restrain by means of legislation those who were inciting to hate and violence. Of course, other factors entered into this particular situation. The members of the committee believed that any action taken to resist the anti-Semites would only increase the venom of the haters. But the significant fact to observe is that this kind of one-sided and truncated view of the problem has led to the spread of anti-democratic and anti-Christian propaganda, with all its accompanying distress. The proper laws, properly enforced, would have prevented much trouble. Such laws should have been passed, and applied, not only to anti-Semites of the Nazi variety but to all who, even in the name of Christianity, arouse the hatred and suspicion of people against the Jews or other groups.

B. PROTESTANTS AND JEWS VS. CATHOLICS

Let us now turn our attention to the

alleged grievances directed against the Catholics. . . . 1. The relation of Catholics to the Pope of Rome is regarded as involving a divided political allegiance. . . . 2. The maintenance of parochial schools believed to be divisive and un-American in their influence, together with the effort to secure state aid for them. . . . 3. The political ambitions and solidarity of the Catholic Church. . . . 4. The reluctance of Catholic leaders to coöperate with Protestant forces in community enterprises and the solution of social problems. . . . 5. The idea that Catholics believe Protestants cannot be saved. . . .

The first two charges, dealing with the relation of the Catholics to the Pope, and the parochial schools, have been examined at length in earlier sections. I shall therefore proceed directly to the third charge.

3. *Political ambition and solidarity:* This charge against the Catholics would imply that Catholics tend to direct undue attention to the affairs of state, and to seek to control the offices or the officers of high administrative influence, in order to mold the political life of the nation in accordance with a Catholic program of action. Stated simply, non-Catholics are afraid that the Catholics wish to gain control of the government and then to run it according to orders received from Rome.

Obviously, this charge is another way of stating the first, namely, that Catholics stand in a relation to the Pope which involves a divided political allegiance; and that charge, in turn, relates to the entire problem of religious groups with foreign homelands. For the sake of economy, the reader is referred to those pages above where the problem is discussed.

4. *Catholic non-coöperation:* The National Conference is quite correct in stating that the reluctance to work together with Protestant forces in community enterprises "varies with localities." Yet, within the limits of those variations, Catholics may be praised or blamed according as they fulfill the terms of the ethical principle. If their lack of coöperation should ever assume proportions which jeopardized the unity of the

whole (whether city, country, state, or nation), the situation would be intolerable. But so long as the equilibrium is not upset, the individuality of the Catholic group must be defended.

5. *Protestants cannot be saved:* Non-Catholics, since they believe that Catholic doctrines have no bearing on their lives, need not be disturbed by the refusal of Catholics to believe that God will save them. If non-Catholics do not accept the Catholic system of salvation, they cannot be affected by it: being rejected should not depress them and being accepted should not elate them.

This charge is meaningless to Catholics, and should be meaningless to non-Catholics. Non-Catholics should realize that for them the Catholic doctrine is irrelevant, just as is the traditional Jewish doctrine to nonbelieving Jews. A Rabbinic dictum says, "He who denies the divine authorship of the Torah has no share in the world to come." Obviously, if one does not accept the Torah as divine, one does not take seriously the concept of the world to come which it teaches.

It is difficult to understand, therefore, why the doctrine "No salvation outside the Church" should be a source of tension between Catholics and non-Catholics. One can understand why Catholics should be upset that non-Catholics do not accept Catholic doctrine. But for non-Catholics to consider the Catholic view a source of tension would be reasonable only if the Catholic Church attempted to institute political, economic, or other disabilities affecting non-Catholics. In that event, the source of tension would be the institution of the disabilities, and not the reasons therefor.

C. CATHOLICS AND PROTESTANTS VS. JEWS

"In the same fashion, among the causes of intergroup irritations contributed by the Jewish group, there are alleged: 1. The proportion of objectionable and overaggressive Jews. . . . 2. Prevalent unethical business practices. . . . 3. The undue and growing economic power of Jews, and their crowding of particular professions. . . . 4. A tendency toward political and social radicalism. . . . 5. Internationalism involving a lack of patriotism." Thus *The American Way* presents the case against the Jews as formulated by Catholics and Protestants.

Of the five charges, three have some relevance to the problem of equity: the third, fourth, and fifth. To what extent should individuals, generally, be permitted to increase their economic power, without interference? To what extent should radicalism be permitted? To what extent should international affiliations be tolerated? These questions lend themselves to treatment by the application of the principle of equity, but their consideration belongs properly to another study, one which does not confine itself to religious groups.

Certainly, in view of the facts, there is no particular point in discussing them with relation to the Jews, because even if the charges applied to the Jews more than to other groups, the Jews could not be considered in the discussion as a religious group. The Jews referred to in these charges are not those who adhere to a particular religious denomination but rather those who by accident of birth are identified with the Jewish group. Where discipline within a religious group is lax, such mistakes are bound to happen. Individuals are identified with groups that have no desire to claim them. Protestants suffer a great deal from that circumstance, men who are shown to be neither Catholics nor Jews being generally listed as Protestants.

A legitimate criticism brought against the Jewish religious groups is that they desire to perpetuate themselves as a permanent minority within the framework of the democratic state. The pros and cons of this problem were discussed in the second chapter and the reader is referred to those pages.

But unfortunately, in most good-will work, the distinction is rarely drawn between those who derive from the ethnic group known as Jews and those who represent a specifically Jewish religious system of salvation. An elementary prerequisite for a proper application of the principle of equity is that in discussions of relations between various religious groups only those people be included who belong to such groups, who live in accordance with, or profess, the teachings and the programs of their groups.

D. PROSELYTIZING AMONG VARIOUS RELIGIOUS GROUPS

One of the most common sources of friction between religious groups is the practice of proselytizing. Practically all Christian denominations function on the assumption that their system of beliefs and practices must sooner or later be universally accepted. Spokesmen for these religious groups assert that the ambition to convert is a necessary corollary of the belief in the truth of their religions. The possessor of religious truth is obliged not only to live by the truth but, equally, obliged to share it with others.

It has been said that this attitude is the mother of intolerance. As soon as men began to believe that there was only one way to salvation, namely, their own, they began to convert their fellow men; and when conversion through peaceful suasion failed, other means were resorted to. Political, economic, and social sanctions were applied; and sometimes the torch had to be applied.

Although religious groups in contemporary America are no longer inclined to use force, they are nevertheless committed to the fundamental proposition, from which they have not deviated. That proposition is that their respective religions are the only true ones, or, at least, are possessed of such an overwhelming degree of the truth that salvation for the whole of society will not be achieved until the whole of society is converted to the true faith.

The Christian Church is still committed to the proposition that Christianity must become the religion of all mankind before we can hope to see the world perfected. "The Gospel is the only way of salvation. . . . Its very nature forbids us to say that it may be the right belief for some, but not for others." Unless all become Christians and teach the truths of the "life complete and abundant" on the basis of the Christian Gospels, they cannot be said to have qualified for true salvation.

To be sure, "rays" from the "light" have penetrated even non-Christian religions; but partial faith is not sufficient. "All the good of which men have conceived is fulfilled and secured in Christ": Christianity is, in the words of one Christian leader, not a religion, but *religion*.[4]

Most Christian denominations, therefore, continue to subsidize missions. The greater proportion of missionary energy is expended on foreign soil; but a good deal is directed toward converting unbelievers who are to be found close at hand. This missionary activity creates friction. Those who are missionized call the missionizers "intolerant", and those who missionize regard as intolerant the people who resist them.

Strangely enough the friction is caused by the non-proselytizing attitude as well as by the proselytizing attitude. The Jews in the United States have been criticized as exclusive and particularistic because of their refusal to engage in proselytizing. The Jews theoretically are a missionary people. Traditionally, Judaism looked forward to achieving spiritual hegemony over the whole world. The Messianic era was pictured as one in which everyone would be a Jew. In modern times, the Orthodox movement retained this Messianic hope in the liturgy but permitted its implications to lapse into desuetude. The Reformist movement, however, swore public allegiance to the ideal of Israel's Mission; but, truth to tell, no program was ever worked out to implement the terms of the mission. For practical purposes, Judaism is not a missionary religion.

The only group in Jewish life that has articulated a rationale for this unwillingness to proselytize the Gentiles is the Reconstructionist group, which has clarified its reasons somewhat as follows: Religion is an aspect of a culture or a civilization. It is the self-consciousness of a group expressed in that group's orientation to the cosmos, to society as a whole, to history. The religion of a group is the unique articulation, in terms of the historic experience of the group, of those values which constitute its highest ideals. The values which a group cherishes and the means which it provides for the realization of those values constitute the "salvation" it offers its adherents. The rites, ceremonies, and liturgy which the group develops are the individual and nontransferable expressions of the ideals and values. The ideals and values occupy the realm of universals.

Now, according to the Reconstructionists, religious groups are not necessarily different from one another; they may be just "other." If, for example, the values cherished by two groups are for the most part the same, the groups cannot be said to differ. Yet the groups are not identical. They are other, as two individuals who agree may be other: each believes in filial love, and each loves another father—his own. Two religious groups may believe in freedom; each may derive that belief from a similar view of life and express that belief in the celebration of festivals distinctive and unique. But while the first draws its inspiration from one historic experience, and the second derives inspiration from another history, they may see eye to eye with regard to the values accepted.

Since, however, sancta are susceptible of a variety of interpretations, it is possible to find members of the same group sharing the same sancta but differing as to their values. Contemporaneous adherents of a religion may differ in their ethical valuations, invoking the same authority for both valuations. Certainly, contemporary thinkers often accept in the name of sancta values which were denounced by other thinkers, past and present, in the name of the same sancta.

The problem of proselytism, therefore, for the Reconstructionists, should be approached from an entirely different point of view. They hold that the adoption of new values does not require conversion. Since ethical ideals are universal, they can be incorporated into any system and sanctified by the sancta of that system. There is no need to give up one's whole tradition, associations, social environment, sancta, if one happens to find in another religion values which are more appealing. By assimilation and appropriation, these values can be made part of one's own civilization and religion.

The mistake generally made is in thinking that the universalism of a religion inheres in the adoption of that religion—values, sancta, and all—by all mankind. The universalism of a religion adheres in the universal applicability of its values. Proselytism, therefore, consists—or should consist—in getting others to accept one's values, not one's cultural patterns or one's ancestors and history.

This kind of proselytism meets the objection of those who deny that one religion is as good as another. One religion is certainly better than another insofar as one religion advocates values which are superior to the values advocated by another. It is meaningless to say that the sancta of one religion are better than the sancta of another. The fact is that the sancta of one religion are invaluable and precious to the members of that religion: and are generally of no value at all to members of another. They may have certain purely esthetic values, but they cannot possibly have the appeal to outsiders which they have to those born and brought up within the group.

On the other hand, proselytism, which includes the adoption of sancta as well as values, is a wholesome procedure—for those who wish to throw in their lot completely with the members of another group. If a man wishes to marry a member of another religious group, he certainly should become completely assimilated into that group. He may find that the values cherished in the new group are no different from those on which he was brought up; but in the new environment, in order to express a loyalty to those values, he must talk the "language" of his new coreligionists.

This is a strange reversal. In former times, conversion for the purpose of marrying a member of another faith was considered less meritorious than conversion on the basis of the recognition that another religion was better. From the Reconstructionist point of view, conversion because of the recognition of a better set of values is needless, while conversion in order to integrate oneself into another cultural pattern is altogether fitting.

The relation of the foregoing discussion to our problem of tolerance and the application of the principle of equity should be quite clear. When an attempt is made by a religious group to proselytize the members of another group, the following question should be asked: To what extent is the proselytizing group attempting to induce others to adopt a different set of values, and to what extent is it trying to get the members of another group to exchange their sancta for a different set of sancta? If the purpose is to impress upon others the superiority of a set of values, the religious group is satisfying the requirements of the principle of equity, for it is seeking to effect an agreement in those areas where agreement makes for coöperation without affecting individuality. If, on the other hand, the purpose is to effect a surrender of sancta in exchange for other sancta, the principle of equity is violated, for in this instance individuality is discouraged, with no necessary effect upon coöperation.

By confining missionary work to the realm of ideas, of values and of ethical standards, religious groups could avoid the friction which results from proselytizing activities and at the same time satisfy their desire to seek universality for the content of their respective religions. If, however, religious groups refuse to accept the Reconstructionist interpretation, and insist that ideas and values are so completely involved with sancta as to render dissociation impossible or meaningless, and that conversion can only mean discarding the old way of life, with its associations, memories, emotional ties, and system of values, then we must face the problem in the same way as that suggested with regard to the secular faiths. We must recognize the right of one religious group, historic or secular, to convert the members of other groups to the "true" religion, providing that due care is taken to preserve the right to individuality on the part of those who wish to retain their original religious affiliations, and to preserve the unity of the entire community against those who might jeopardize it through their missionary zeal.

NOTES AND REFERENCES

CHAPTER I

1. See *World Fellowship,* p. 10 and p. 31.
2. The factual history of inter-faith cooperation during the 1920's is taken from *Catholics, Jews and Protestants,* by Claris Edwin Silcox and Galen M. Fisher. (Hereafter, this book will be referred to as Silcox and Fisher). A complete account of the history of the inter-faith movement in the United States is also given in the *Universal Jewish Encyclopedia,* New York, 1940; article "Better Understanding Between Jews and Christians."
3. Silcox and Fisher, p. 331.
4. *All in the Name of God,* Chapter I.
5. Silcox and Fisher, p. v.
6. Ibid., Chapter IX.
7. *The Saturday Evening Post* of June 1, 1940 carried a lengthy article by Stanley High entitled "Satan, Be Warned," describing inter-faith activities in the United States.
8. Silcox and Fisher, p. 308.
9. Silcox and Fisher, p. 311. High scores for achievement in stimulating the assumption of "common tasks for the general good," and thus contributing to the "removal of ignorance and its evil progeny . . . mutual distrust, friction and schism . . ." are granted to the National Conference of Christians and Jews, the Community Chests and Councils of Social Agencies, the united staffs and programs at various universities, and the North American Board for the Study of Religion in Higher Education.
10. The Council Against Intolerance in America is a comparatively new organization, dedicated, as the name reveals, to combatting intolerance in all its forms. It has published an educational manual entitled "An American Answer to Intolerance," which is distributed for use in Junior and Senior High Schools. The manual seeks to fight intolerance by: (a) analyzing propaganda, as a means toward helping people to detect it and thus to nullify its evil effects; (b) supplying accurate information about various national and racial groups: (This work is similar to that of the National Conference, except that the Conference works through the colleges, and the Council in the high schools.) (c) calling attention to American ideals, and reaffirming them; (d) stimulating self-examination for prejudice and habitual attitudes.

    We're All Americans is the title of a second manual prepared for use in elementary schools by the Council.
11. Silcox and Fisher, quoting Roger W. Straus, one of the co-chairmen of the organization.
12. Quoted in the "report of the Director," Nov. 2, 1939.
13. *Ten Years of Inter-faith Work,* by Everett R. Clinchy, Director, N.C.C.J., Dec. 29, 1937, published by the N.C.C.J. News Service, New York. The National Conference of Jews and Christians became the National Conference of Christians and Jews in November, 1938. This explains why it is referred to sometimes as N.C.C.J., and at others as N.C.J.C.

14. *Religion, A Digest*, Vol. 2, No. 1, (Nov. 1939), p. 93. This issue of *Religion* is devoted exclusively to reporting the proceedings of the Institute of Human Relations held at Williamstown, Mass., during the summer of 1939. Every paper delivered there is published here in abbreviated form.

15. *Religious Liberty and Democracy*, by Roger Williams Straus, p. 70.

16. Ibid., p. 70.

17. It is interesting to note that some workers in the field of good will have a tendency to cavalierly disregard ideological differences. In speaking of the same three groups, Straus says further (ibid. p. 81) that: "Each in its own way is endeavoring to reach men's souls and hearts, to make them better, and to go forward to that common ideal of all modern religions, the fatherhood of God and the brotherhood of man." It is highly questionable whether the Protestants, or the Catholics, or the Jews would be willing to agree that basically they were all alike. Even to say that they are all *striving* for the same thing ignores the fact that one group may claim to have achieved it, and that all others have failed. This negligible little item seems to play no part in Straus' pollyannish treatment. He follows the same line in describing the Jews. He insists (ibid. p. 99) that differences of Orthodox, Conservative and Reform Jews are only "superficial to meet individual viewpoints as to methods." An honest study of the ideological differences reveals that more than "viewpoints as to methods" are at stake. This tendency to assume that there is a *common denominator to all various groups* in their religious ideology is one type of highly inadequate approach to the general problem.

18. Louis Minsky, "Ten Years of Good Will," *Frater*, Vol. XX, No. 1 (October 1937).

19. *Intolerance*, by Winfred Ernest Garrison.

20. Ibid., p. 267.

21. Ibid., p. 259.

22. Ibid., p. 259.

23. Ibid., p. 262.

24. Ibid., p. 267.

25. Roger W. Straus, in *Religious Liberty and Democracy*, in the chapter entitled "Religious Liberty—Civilization's Barometer," traces the rise and fall of political and economic prosperity in various countries, and indicates a high correlation between a flourishing state and the practice of tolerance. He nullifies his whole analysis, however, when he states, (p. 17): "As yet I have been unable to determine whether it is a cause or an effect." *The Reconstructionist*, Vol. I. No. 14, (Nov. 15, 1935), commenting on Straus' essay, remarks wisely: "If religious liberty were the cause of an expanding civilization, we should know at once how to bring about recovery. If it were the effect, we should stop preaching about it and proceed to reconstruct the social order, letting the effect follow the cause naturally."

26. *Judaism in Transition*, by Mordecai M. Kaplan. All quotations from Kaplan in this section are found in Chapter IX.

27. See Note 4.

28. Clinchy, Chapter XIV.

29. Ibid., p. 165.

30. Ibid., pp. 165-166; pp. 176-177; p. 152.

31. The Fellowship of Faiths articulated the slogan: "Unity in variety, not uniformity"; and the University Religious Conference declared its motto to be: "Cooperation without compromise"; but at no point did these groups elaborate the implications of their slogans or mottos. They simply expressed a concept whose basic foundations they did not examine, or whose sociological or ethical implications they did not explore. They did not even make clear that they were touching upon a vital distinction between what they were doing and what the other tolerance-groups were trying to accomplish; namely, to distinguish between the friction that exists as a result of unwarranted fear and hate, and that which results from legitimate fear. They were not aware that they were unconsciously groping for a formula which would take cognizance of differences, the true nature of which all parties were aware of, and avowedly accepted.

32. Silcox and Fisher, p. 352; p. 347. Cf. "Christianity in This Hour," by George N. Shuster, from *Survey Graphic*, Feb. 1939. "Such differences are not evil in themselves. They add a great deal, at least potentially, to the vitality and interest of the national life. We can profit, if we like, by French refinement and Irish wit; by Yankee shrewdness and Negro willingness to sing and bear it. An American may, if he so desires, study the religions of all the world without leaving home, sample the products of every school of cookery, and hear all the tongues of earth in turn. If variety be truly the spice of life, there is lack of nothing to whet our appetites."

33. Clinchy, p. 167.

34. Silcox and Fisher, p. 353.

35. Issue of July 7, 1937.

36. Cf. Peter Harlow, *The Shortest Way With the Jews*. London, George Allen and Unwin Ltd., 1939. Harlow goes further, urging tolerance as a method of precipitating homogeneity. "There is only one solution for the Jews outside Palestine: absorption. There is only one way of achieving this aim: tolerance." pp. 236-237.

37. Clinchy, p. 177.

38. Quoted by Silcox and Fisher, p. 355; p. 357.

39. Ibid., p. 357.

40. *The American Hebrew*, Sept. 8, 1939.

CHAPTER II

1. *Reason and Nature*, by Morris Raphael Cohen, Chapter IV, Section V.

2. *The Hope of the Great Community*, by Josiah Royce, pp. 43, 51-52, 54. See also his *The Problem of Christianity*, New York, The Macmillan Co., 1913. Chapter III particularly.

3. *Systems of Strife and Productive Duality*, by Wilmon Henry Sheldon.

4. Sheldon, p. 528.

5. Ibid., p. 521.

6. Ibid., p. 445.

7. In medicine, the human body is said to have a "tolerance" for a chemical when that chemical does not upset the normal equilibrium of the body.

8. *The American Stakes*, by John Chamberlain.

9. Ibid., pp. 31-32.

10. Ibid., p. 282.

11. *Of Human Freedom*, by Jacques Barzun.

12. Ibid., p. 19.

13. Sheldon, p. 520.

14. Cf. John Dewey, *Freedom and Culture*, pp. 21-22. "Human nature, like other forms of life, tends to differentiation, and . . . it also tends toward combination, association. . . . Some cultural conditions develop the psychological constituents that lead toward differentiation; others stimulate those which lead in the direction of the solidarity of the beehive or anthill. The human problem is that of securing the development of each constituent so that it serves to release and mature the other. Cooperation is as much a part of the democratic ideal as is personal initiative."

15. *The City of Man, a Declaration on World Democracy*, p. 33. Cf. also p. 26.

16. New York, Vanguard Press, Inc., 1940.

17. Cf. Ludwig Lewisohn's distinction between "identical rights" and "equivalent rights" in *The Answer*, New York, Liveright Publishing Corp., 1939. Also H. W. Schneider's critique of "equivalent rights," *Ethics*, Vol. 50, No. 1 (Oct. 1939).

18. "The inquisitors of all times appear as the vindicators of public morality." *God in Freedom*, by Luigi Luzzatti, p. 5.

19. Cf. *The American Way*, A Study of Human Relations amongst Protestants, Catholics and Jews, Chapter II. "Human Relations: Lessons from other lands. What can *we* learn from Germany?" p. 15. "The first lesson that we in this country may learn from contemporary events in Germany is the necessity that all who believe in God and in a spiritual interpretation of life's meaning must stand together for those convictions which they hold in common, lest they be dissipated or destroyed by the pervasive influences in the modern world that deny them. . . ."

    Cf. also *The Church and the Political Problem of Our Day*, by Karl Barth, p. 21. Barth favors a united front of the Church with "even liberals, Jews and Marxists" to fight the common enemy, "National Socialism."

20. *Theories of Americanization*: A critical study, with Special Reference to the Jewish Group, by Isaac B. Berkson.

21. Berkson, p. 91.

22. Ibid., p. 122.

23. The Common Council for American Unity, which began the publication in the Fall of 1940 of a magazine, *Common Ground*, and which plans an ambitious program (according to a prospectus which appeared in June 1940) concerns itself with the problem of inter-ethnic and inter-racial intolerance. The Council will strive to encourage "Unity Within Diversity." "In this fear-burdened, war-torn world, the danger of a unity that insists on uniformity is all too real. In contrast, the Common Council for American Unity

believes that the only enduring unity can come from permitting differences, from accepting each other as we are. There must, to be sure, be a common belief in democracy and the ideals of liberty. On these basic principles there can be no compromise. But within the circle of such a common belief, the freedom to be different is not only the only policy consistent with democracy and liberty, but the one most likely to bring out the basic sameness of people. Unity within diversity is the strongest amalgam we can make. By welcoming differences, encouraging an appreciation of what each group can and has contributed to the interests of any group, the Common Council believes that most can be done to eliminate prejudice on the one hand, and humiliation on the other, to give us all a feeling of pride in our backgrounds and a sense of identification with the United States, to promote harmony and fusion—in short, to bring about a real and enduring unity."

A careful reading of the Prospectus, from which the above is quoted, does not reveal clearly whether the C.C.A.U. favors heterogeneity as well as homogeneity. To be sure, it stresses the values of difference, but again and again mention is made of the failure of the *melting pot* in not having taken into it all the elements in American life. The word "fusion" is also somewhat ambiguous. That ultimately a homogeneous population is envisaged is quite apparent. What is not so clear is the extent to which varieties of distinctive cultural self-expression will be encouraged. In any case, the general tone of the Council is wholesome, and its work should be observed with interest.

Compare also the work of the Service Bureau for Inter-cultural Relations, in New York.

24. Cf. "I don't want to Christianize the world!" by Charles T. Holman, *Christian Century*, Nov. 20, 1935; and the reply, "Do I want to Christianize the World? Yes!" by Charles Clayton Murreson, Nov. 27, 1935.

25. Cf. "The Small Community Within the Large," by S. H. Markowitz, *Religious Education*, Vol. 35, No. 2. (April-June 1940), pp. 83-88.

"Speech is a universal experience; yet we have many languages. Religion is a universally human product; yet we have many religions." Rabbi Markowitz adds some interesting data regarding "cultural pluralism" in action.

26. Cf. *Freedom and Culture*, by John Dewey. "Exegesis can always serve to bridge gaps and inconsistencies; and every absolutistic creed demonstrates that no limits can be put to exegetical ingenuity. What actually happens can, accordingly, be brought into harmony with dogma while the latter is covertly accommodated to events."

27. *The Nature of the Judicial Process*, by Benjamin N. Cardozo. New Haven, Yale University Press, 1924, p. 47.

28. *Jurisprudence*, by Munroe Smith, quoted by Cardozo, p. 23.

CHAPTER III

1. Cf. *Things That Are Caesar's*, by Paul B. Means. He tells of Protestantism in Germany before the World War as conceiving of the church as exercising purely spiritual functions, presiding over the inner life, and concerned

solely with the salvation of the soul; whereas the state was viewed as the master of all external, secular affairs, and the controller of public morality.

Cf. also: "Religion is man's belief in a power upon which he depends, to which he is obligated and with which he may commune, together with the activities arising from the belief." Compared to democracy, religion is man's relationship "to God; in the other (democracy) to his fellowmen. . . . Religion is in essence the relation of the individual to his conscience through God." Straus, *Religious Liberty*, pp. 61-62.

2. Cf. *Judaism in a Changing Civilization*, by Samuel Dinin. New York. Teachers College, 1931, pp. 85-88. Dinin shows how the state-supported schools have gradually assumed responsibility for the teaching of all those subjects formerly taught under the general category of "religion."

Cf. also Daniel L. Marsh, of Boston University, who has written *The American Canon*, approaching "Americanism" as a religion. "I felt," he writes in his Introduction, "the need of something that . . . all Americans would accept as the undisputed creed, or 'Bible' of Americanism." His selections from the writings of great Americans are designed to offer the "Genesis," "Exodus," "Law," "Prophets," "Psalms," "Gospels," and "Epistles," of the American "Bible."

Cf. *Church and State in Contemporary America*, by William Adams Brown. He quotes Christopher Dawson: "What modern Christians have to fear is not the danger of violent persecution but rather that of the crushing out of religion from modern life by the sheer weight of a state-inspired public opinion, and by the mass organization of society on a purely secular basis." (p. 16) Dawson should, more correctly, have said that the state is tending to become the rival of the church for the religious loyalty of the people; the state is itself an institution functioning as a religion, and to call it "secular" is merely to call it names. Harry Emerson Fosdick correctly stated (*New York Times*, May 27, 1940) "Stalinism, fascism and nazism are all religions, competitive with Christianity."

3. Cf. Means, ibid., pp. 97 ff., and also Brown, ibid., pp. 9 ff.

4. Cf. Karl Barth, ibid., p. 41. "And now National Socialism, according to its own revelation of what it is,—a self-revelation to which it has devoted all the time and chance till now allowed—is as well without any doubt something quite different from a political experiment. It is, namely, *a religious institution of salvation.*"

5. For a full discussion of sancta and their place in religion, see *Judaism As A Civilization*, by Mordecai M. Kaplan, pp. 319 ff.; 519 ff.

CHAPTER IV

1. The most comprehensive presentation of the problems involved in this question is to be found in *Religious Education*, Vol. XXXV, No. 4 (October-December 1940). Harrison S. Elliot and a small group of religious educators prepared a Suggested Syllabus on Religious Education and Public Education (Part 1 dealing with elementary and secondary education, and

Part 2, prepared by Stewart G. Cole, dealing with higher education). This syllabus includes discussion and bibliography on: I. The Present Situation; II. Suggested Ways of Meeting the Problem; III. Basic Differences and Underlying Issues for Further Exploration; IV. Coming to a Decision.

2. *Church and State*, pp. 119-122.

3. Cf. Luther A. Weigle, *Public Education and Religion*, International Council of Religious Education, 1940. Dean Weigle pleads for the teaching of "the religious faith of the American people," the "common religious faith."

4. Teachers Guild Associates, (mimeographed), 1941. See also F. Ernest Johnson, *The Social Gospel Re-examined*, New York, Harper & Bros., 1940, pp. 187-191.

    Cf. Harrison S. Elliot's plea for introducing courses in public schools leading to "religious literacy" on the part of the students. *Religious News Service*, 5/13/41.

5. Cf. John Dewey, as reported in the *New York Times*, Nov. 14, 1940. "They (the men who made the Constitution) knew that the introduction of religious differences in American life would undermine the democratic foundations of this country. What holds for adults holds even more for children, sensitive and conscious of differences."

6. In October 1940 President Butler of Columbia University, amid criticism, made a similar plea for the rights of a university to *its* freedom.

7. An excellent summation of the various views expressed on the Russell case pro and con, by the press, the pulpit, the academicians, politicians, etc., is contained in the American Committee for Democracy and Intellectual Freedom's *News Service*, March 23, 1940, entitled "Free Thought and Free Thinking—The Bertrand Russell Case." The issue of April 15, 1940 continues the publication of facts concerning the Russell case, and includes also some data on the question of "Religion in Education," which are relevant to our discussion above.

CHAPTER V

1. *New York Times*, March 25, 1941.

2. *New York Times*, March 13, 1940. Cf. "The Taylor Appointment," by Rev. J. Elliott Ross, *Religious News Service*, May 31, 1940.

3. Silcox and Fisher, p. 356.

4. *The American* Way, pp. 35-36.

CHAPTER VI

1. "In Defense of Democracy," by Frank Murphy. *International Conciliation*, No. 360, (May 1940).

2. *Reason and Nature*, p. 378.

3. Herbert W. Schneider, in *The American Scholar*, Summer, 1940, discusses Ascoli's article on free speech in the previous issue. He asks for a "police-

man" to intervene "in the interests of fair competition." I question, however, whether it is enough to have "enough soap boxes to go around" in order to insure free competition. Competition, to be free, must be honest.

Incidentally, compare *Ethics of the Fathers*, Chapter V, par. 20: "Every controversy which is for the sake of Heaven will in the end be established. Every one which is not for the sake of Heaven will not in the end be established."

4. *Freedom: Its Meaning*, edited by Ruth Nanda Anshen, p. 332.
5. Ibid., p. 255.
6. Ibid., p. 254.
7. *Moral Man and Immoral Society*, p. 175.
8. *American Scholar*, Summer, 1940.

CHAPTER VII

1. *The American Way*, pp. 34-38.
2. The sect of Jehovah's Witnesses has certainly confused matters. For them, nationalism even in its symbolic form—the flag—is the enemy of religion, and a salute to the flag is idolatry. The Supreme Court of the United States, on June 3, 1940, had to insist that members of that group salute and pay due reverence to the flag, or suffer penalization. Unfortunately, members of other denominations interpreted that decision as an encouragement to pogromize the Witnesses; but from the point of view of equity, the judges were right, since in the nation as a whole the outstanding "symbol of our national unity" cannot be repudiated without implying the repudiation of coöperation, and the upset of equilibrium.
3. *American Jewish Year Book*, Vol. 35 (1936-37), pp. 224-225. On Jan. 7, 1941, the constitutionality of a New Jersey law was upheld, which law prohibits incitement to racial or religious hatred. (*New York Times*, Jan. 8, 1941).
4. Quotations are from *The Christian Life and Message in Relation to Non-Christian Systems of Thought and Life*, Vol. I, Chapter XIII, "The Christian Message." Cf. *The World Mission of the Church*, 1939, pp. 20-21.

SELECTED BIBLIOGRAPHY

The American Way, A Study of Human Relations among Protestants, Catholics and Jews. Edited by Newton Diehl Baker, Carlton J. H. Hayes and Roger Williams Straus. New York, Willett, Clark & Co., 1936.

Barth, Karl. The Church and the Political Problem of Our Day. New York, Charles Scribner's Sons, 1939.

Barzun, Jacques. Of Human Freedom. Boston, Little, Brown & Co., 1939.

Berkson, Isaac B. Theories of Americanization. New York, Teachers College, 1920.

Brown, William Adams. Church and State in Contemporary America. New York, Charles Scribner's Sons, 1936.

Chamberlain, John. The American Stakes. New York, J. B. Lippincott Co., 1940.

The Christian Life and Message in Relation to Non-Christian Systems of Thought and Life, Vol. I. New York, International Missionary Council, 1928.

Christians and Jews, a Reading List. Compiled by Benson Y. Landis. New York, National Conference of Christians and Jews, 1940.

The City of Man: A Declaration of World Democracy. New York, Viking Press, Inc., 1940.

Clinchy, Everett R. All in the Name of God. New York, The John Day Co., 1934.

Cohen, Morris Raphael. Reason and Nature. New York, Harcourt, Brace & Co., Inc., 1931.

Common Ground, a periodical, edited by Louis Adamic. New York, Common Council for American Unity.

Dewey, John. Freedom and Culture. New York, G. P. Putnam's Sons, 1939.

Freedom: Its Meaning. Edited by Ruth Nanda Anshen. New York, Harcourt, Brace & Co., Inc., 1940.

Garrison, Winfred E. Intolerance. New York, Round Table Press, Inc., 1934.

Jews in America. Edited by the editors of Fortune. New York, Random House, Inc., 1936.

Kaplan, Mordecai M. Judaism As A Civilization. New York, The Macmillan Co., 1934.

Kaplan, Mordecai M. Judaism In Transition. New York, Covici, Friede, Inc., 1936.

Landman, Isaac. Christian and Jew. New York, Horace Liveright, 1929.

Luzzatti, Luigi. God in Freedom. New York. The Macmillan Co., 1930.

Marsh, Daniel L. The American Canon. New York, Abingdon-Cokesbury Press, 1939.

Means, Paul B. Things That Are Caesar's. New York, Round Table Press, Inc., 1935.

Moehlman, Conrad H. The Christian-Jewish Tragedy. Rochester, Leo Hart, 1933.

Murphy, Frank. "In Defense of Democracy." American Council on Public Affairs, Washington, D. C.

Niebuhr, Reinhold. Moral Man and Immoral Society: A Study in Ethics and Politics. New York, Charles Scribner's Sons, 1932.

Perry, Ralph Barton. . . . Shall Not Perish From the Earth. New York, Vanguard Press, Inc., 1940.

Royce, Josiah. The Hope of the Great Community. New York, The Macmillan Co, 1916.

Sheldon, Wilmon Henry. Strife of Systems and Productive Duality: An Essay in Philosophy. Cambridge, Harvard University Press, 1918.

Silcox, Claris Edwin, and Fisher, Galen M. Catholics, Jews and Protestants. New York, Harper & Bros., 1934.

Straus, Roger Williams. Religious Liberty and Democracy. Chicago, Willett, Clark & Co., 1939.

Van Loon, Hendrik. Tolerance. New York. Boni & Liveright, 1925. (Revised edition, 1940).

We Americans. Boston, Atlantic Monthly, 1939.

Wise, James Waterman, and Levinger, Lee Joseph. Mr. Smith, Meet Mr. Cohen. New York, Reynal & Hitchcock, Inc., 1940.

World Fellowship. Edited by Charles Frederick Weller. New York, Liveright Publishing Corp., 1935.

Bei Fragen zur Produktsicherheit wenden Sie sich bitte an:
If you have any questions regarding product safety,
please contact:

Walter de Gruyter GmbH
Genthiner Straße 13
10785 Berlin
productsafety@degruyterbrill.com